For a great many years, I have been privileged to know and work with John Cerbone. As I am both a psychoanalyst and teacher, John has revolutionized my practice with his formidable training in a wide variety of hypnotic techniques.

From his groundbreaking innovative insights on hypnotic suggestion, to his intensive speed inductions training program, the methods John has taught me have greatly enhanced my effectiveness clinically. These new insights have been an invaluable breakthrough in assisting members of the armed forces effected by post-traumatic stress disorders.

John Cerbone is an extraordinarily sensitive, dynamic and creative pleasure to know and have as part of my world, both professionally and personally. This new book is a revolutionary masterwork of hypnotic suggestion, which I am certain will be of enormous benefit to the entirety of hypnotic professionals worldwide.

Lilith Martin, PhD, MA, CI

Endorsements for
Power Hypnosis Insights

"Insight. John Cerbone uses this word throughout the book *Power Hypnosis - The Future of Hypnotic Sessions - Insights and Suggestions* to help the reader master the techniques and approaches of hypnosis. But this book is a real insight into almost 40 years of experience, which John Cerbone brings to the reader in a clear, concise, practice and straightforward way. Do you want a solid foundation for understanding hypnosis? Are you an advanced practitioner who wants to refine your own work? Are you new to hypnotherapy and want to make sure you really understand hypnosis and the subconscious mind? Then this book is for you."

Dr. Richard Nongard
Author of *Speak Ericksonian: Mastering the Hypnotic Methods of Milton Erickson*

A must-have for any professional hypnotist, This awesome book is not only comprehensive and concise, but also gives the reader updated and redefined interdisciplinary approaches to understanding how the mind and hypnosis combines. This masterpiece uncovers the secrets of the masters and some will even say it is one up the newest Bibles of Hypnotism.

Capt. Bill Pettek BCH, CI

John, The Trance Master, as he is known, brings his insight and experience to the forefront in his great new book. This work is a great read for the newcomer or those who have been in the field for a while. Get this book if you are serious about hypnosis as profession!

Will Horton, Psy.D. CAC
World's Leading NLP Trainer
www.drwillhorton.com
www.nfnlp.com

John Cerbone's third book, *Power Hypnosis – The Future of Hypnotic Sessions* is an excellent guide to leading-edge hypnosis suggestion and theory. A well-known innovator in the field, Cerbone's techniques serve to advance traditional methods. I recommend this book to all professional clinical hypnotists and hypnotherapists who wish to improve client outcomes.

Deborah Miller, BS, BCH
www.HypnosisCanHelp.Me

"Every once in a while someone comes along in the fields of science, physics, psychology, and medicine whose work and creative insights initiate a paradigm shift. **John Cerbone is that kind of someone, and his book *Power Hypnosis – The Future of Hypnotic Sessions* reflects his work and creative hypnotic insights that will initiate such a paradigm shift in the field of Hypnotism."

Janice Matturro
http://www.theinnerworkshop.com/

I had the good fortune to see an early draft of this book, and it is unlike any other hypnosis book I've ever seen. Not a collection of scripts, it reveals insights and suggestions to help hypnotists create their own scripts and tailor them to the needs of individual clients and situations. John developed these insights in the process of becoming one of the most successful hypnotists in North America. I believe we can all learn from his decades of success with this new book.

Robert M Dunscomb
Board Certified Hypnotist

POWER
HYPNOSIS

POWER
HYPNOSIS

THE FUTURE OF HYPNOTIC SESSIONS

Insights and Suggestions

Exclusive Must-Have Insider Secrets for the Next Generation of Successful Hypnotic Breakthroughs

CONCEIVED AND WRITTEN BY

JOHN CERBONE

Certified Professional Hypnotist

ISBN 10: 1933817453

ISBN 13: 978-1-933817-45-3

JOHN CERBONE

Certified Professional Hypnotist
Cerbone Hypnosis Institute
Certified Clinical Hypnotist Instructor

CerboneHypnosisInstitute.com

WorldFamousHypnotist.com

HypnosisStageShow.com

HypnotistPro.com

CONTENTS

FOREWORD

THANK YOU for purchasing my book:

Power Hypnosis - The Future of Hypnotic Sessions
Insights and Suggestions
Exclusive Must-Have Insider Secrets for the Next
Generation of Successful Hypnotic Breakthroughs

Welcome to the next generation of clinical hypnosis. This book represents decades of my work in this field. As a trained Hypnotism Professional, you will quickly come to understand my use of a wide variety of hypnotic techniques, as well as a redefinition of numerous ideas and insights. You will also understand the use of truisms and confusion techniques within these *Insights and Suggestions* to further enhance their impact and long-term effectiveness.

These suggestion techniques are written in the style and language of this profession, including *run-on sentences,* which is the way many Hypnotism Professionals deliver suggestions for greatest impact. All of the original suggestions, techniques and methods contained herein have proven effective and beneficial for the vast majority of clients (patients). Quite often clients have achieved amazing beneficial results in one or just a few sessions.

For a great many Hypnotists utilizing this work, you will very likely find your clients (patients) achieving breakthroughs quite rapidly.

These new insights target a client's weak spots to insure greater lasting, high-impact success. This book is ergonomically designed; the words are intentionally spread out across the pages to make it lighter to carry and thereby easier to use and transport.

Important Notes: As when using any professional tool, it is assumed, understood and hereby agreed to, that you will be pre-reading each of these scripts before using them and that you will make the appropriate adjustments based upon the needs of your client. This book is solely and strictly intended for use *only* by professionals in the field of Hypnotism, including but not necessarily limited to professionally trained and qualified Hypnotists, Clinical Hypnotists, Psychologists, Psychotherapists, Psychoanalysts, Psychiatrists and other skilled Mental Health Professionals who have been properly trained and certified in the use of professional hypnosis/clinical hypnosis. This information is being shared so that people will be helped, lives will be improved and so that the professionals listed above can and will build further benefit and improvement in their invaluable work. It is understood and agreed to, that the user of the methods contained herein holds the author completely free of liability or any kind of indemnity in using this information in any clinical environment or otherwise.

I wish to sincerely thank my clients, my family, loved ones, friends and colleagues for their tireless support and inspiration, which has helped to make this work possible. I wish to thank all of those individuals with whom I have consulted, those I've trained in the numerous workshops I've hosted over the years, all of the practitioners who have gone before me, as well as those who represent the future of this noble profession.

And as a purchaser of this work, I want to sincerely and personally thank you for your interest and support. I truly wish you limitless creative inspiration and unstoppable success in each and every area of your lives.

Sincerely,
John Cerbone
Certified Professional Hypnotist
Board Certified Hypnotist
Certified Clinical Hypnosis Instructor
Master Hypnotist
© 2015 Cerbone Hypnosis Institute

Empowerment Hypnosis Suggestions for Hypnosis Professionals

Optimized Hypnosis

Optimizing Suggestions for Better Breakthrough Outcomes

Inspiring Transformation / Greatness in Your Client Through Suggestion

Welcome to this book!

PART I – PERSONAL INSIGHTS

THIS BOOK is about revolutionizing *your work* as a professional clinical hypnotist and dramatically increasing the results of clinical hypnosis sessions to more fully improve your clients' lives.

Within the course of this work I will share professional insights I have personally developed over my many years of practice to raise the impact of private clinical hypnosis sessions to the next quantum level.

What's my story?

I have been involved in the hypnosis profession for four decades. I love what I do, and as I've been told, I eat, breathe and sleep hypnosis. Each day, I find myself taking time to think and reflect, pondering on ways to improve the hypnosis methods we have been taught.

I remain absolutely determined to actively create and develop new insights and techniques in this wonderful hypnosis profession, ever–improving and evolving upward this powerfully transformative means of improving lives.

Personal Background

First, a little bit of background on me.

I have been actively practicing forms of hypnosis and self-hypnosis since I was three years old. It seems hypnotic techniques were a part of me from a young age.

I can remember being sent up to my room to pick up after myself. Before I was ready to start cleaning, I would first lie down on my bed, breathe deeply, and put myself into what was essentially a hypnotic state. After utilizing my self-developed technique, the room tidying was a bit more effortless and smooth. Afterwards, unlike other neighborhood kids, I didn't seem to have a sore back and leaden legs.

I can recall moments in grammar school, high school and college where classmates would approach me with various life issues and challenges, asking me to help them. I can recall externalizing my self-developed hypnosis techniques by having them sit down, close their eyes, listen to my voice and relax. Upon opening their eyes, they were almost always relieved of their frustrated, angry, or upset condition and would forego doing something incredibly dangerous or regrettably inappropriate.

After college I remember using these techniques occasionally with sales force coworkers for stress reduction and motivation. In one job I was actually training sales people using my self-developed techniques.

Over time, I took my techniques out into the world via workshops to share publicly the many benefits of my methods. Back in those days, I called it "Personal Empowerment Meditation" and I soon built quite a following. My focus was on stress management, relaxation, and healing, to name just a few.

Many people regularly attended and enjoyed these workshops, often bringing friends. I was busy hosting workshop groups, both large and small. Sometimes just a handful of people would attend, other times there were hundreds.

One evening after a rather packed workshop, a man walked up to me and said, "You are one heck of a hypnotist, and I run a hypnosis school. Why not train with me and become certified? You will be able to help more people." I gratefully followed through on his offer. This was the first of dozens of hypnosis training certifications I've earned throughout my long career.

From my earliest training, my goal has been to learn as much as I could from the best people I could find. Throughout my training and my career, I consistently found my mind actively thinking up improvements to generate higher-impact methods. Whenever someone told me there was a limit to how far something could go regarding beneficial effects or more effective techniques, I always sought out ways to push beyond those believed limits to achieve a greater place of habit-improving, life-changing impact.

On the clinical session end of what we do, I initially found much of the early training material I was given lacking to some degree. These often included slow-paced approaches, badly worded suggestions, and especially far too many typographical errors.

With the many various insights I developed over the years and so many certifications and additional training sparking my creativity and insight, I've always appreciated the beauty, impact and wisdom of our hypnotic work, which often succeeded beyond my expectations.

Hypnosis and suggestion are really amazing tools. I have personally witnessed so much benefit and improvement within people's lives. Some of these improvements were quite astounding for the clients! I consider myself privileged to have been an instrument in delivering these changes.

Our essentially priceless work as hypnotists has the power to literally transform people's lives, bringing order from past chaos.

Quite often I have been asked, "How long does hypnosis last?" A better question is: how long will the benefits of clinical hypnosis last? Benefits from a hypnosis session can last a lifetime, favorably adjusting lives away from destructive habits like smoking and overeating, better management of stress, and so very much more. The possibilities seem practically limitless!

I am always striving to develop and maintain a strong sense of what works and what needs to be upgraded to enhance our professional hypnosis sessions. As I see it, and I think you may agree, this forward thinking is the true key to *fostering the next generation of ideas* leading to better methodologies for greater impact and success. This amazing profession will evolve towards greater levels of impact and life improvement—even perhaps improvements not yet seen or yet unimagined. That's exciting! We can help to improve lives one person at a time, one group that time, and with the Internet, all over the world.

Even though the influence of our work is amazing, day-to-day, most of the public has absolutely no idea of the wonderful services a hypnotist can provide. I have personally witnessed profound upgrades and pivotal life changes taking place as old habits are forgiven, released, and reset, and better thoughts, feelings, habits, and reactions immediately take their place to reshape and improve lives.

Most often a clinical hypnotist is the person's last choice, a chance your client is taking, a last attempt at life improvement. We are usually the last line of defense in a client's life. Most people coming to see a hypnotist have tried almost everything else before finding us. Most of these clients happily break through and succeed, sometimes in spite of themselves. Somehow it would be easier if they simply came to us first.

The public knows so little of who we are and what we do, so each hypnotic professional has a crucially important role as a *goodwill ambassador representative* of our profession to the world. This is just one of the many hats a hypnotist wears professionally while running a successful career. I have personally found it works well letting people know who I am and what benefits hypnosis and suggestion can bring. Seems I'm always "talking hypnosis" in a wide variety of places and handing out business cards as often as appropriate. I never leave the house without business cards.

Other aspects of a hypnotist's career include handling phone calls, responding to emails, answering questions and explaining the workings of hypnosis, scheduling appointments, writing sessions and marketing with copywriting as necessary. These are just a few of the wide variety of aspects, to which can be added media appearances, speaking engagements, lectures and demonstrations, not to mention actually hosting our sessions.

I have always felt deeply and personally driven to elevate my work. All of us, as fully committed dedicated professionals, have taken on the life task of seeking to improve optimal outcomes to ever-increasing success. This is only a natural extension of providing our very best. As our profession evolves, our professional commitment will create ever-yielding remarkable improvements.

Concept –
Quantum Mechanics

Have you ever studied quantum mechanics in chemistry or physics? I first learned of quantum mechanics in my high school chemistry class. Keeping things simple, it's bringing energy to the next possible greater level. From what I remember, this field of science involves the discussion of energy states from lower to higher. Ideas and theories in quantum mechanics are generally illustrated graphically either in circles (sort of like ripples in a pond) or in other versions with a chart where arrow-shaped lines go upward or downward. As insights and suggestions evolve, newer and continuing evolution of techniques will yield quantum movement and better results.

My Intent

It is my intent in writing this book to perform this very same quantum upgrade for our entire clinical hypnosis profession, ushering in even more exciting methods results, concepts and ideas, moreover, a profoundly impacting series of long-term results, upgrading all we do to even greater success and maximum effect.

Through the years I have sought in my practice and professional career to continually and perpetually create—or to actually use a wonderful word, *inculcate* (a word we use in hypnosis when we are doing intake work) the ideas and concepts of enhancing clinical sessions to generate even greater impact and improvement.

What I find personally perplexing at times is observing many professionals who become stuck in various approaches from the past with antiquated ideas and perhaps biases—sticking points from their early years of training—and some of these trained professionals are achieving fewer patient transformations.

My Goal

In writing this book, it is my goal to blow these limitations away, freeing up imagination and creativity, using inspiration and insight, while upgrading our collective professional work to inspire new ideas and bring even greater benefit and improvement into the lives of the clients who seek us out. So what new ideas and approaches will your inspirations create after reading this work?

And just in case you're wondering, the suggestions I've written within these pages have often been written while I was in "trance;" "a flow state;" or "in state," in other words, in "my own hypnosis." This is much in the same way I write suggestions when generating hypnotic scripts for my professional client sessions. I have found I am potentially at my very best when in hypnosis. While I'm writing, I'm bringing my very best! The subconscious mind is a powerful place.

My Sincerest Wish

In writing this, my sincerest wish is to generate an evolution upward in our profession, bringing the very best achievable clinical session results to the next highest quantum level so both you and your clients will be working together and achieving more dynamic results simply by a reorientation and expansion of better-written suggestions, methods and insightful thoughts.

We are Standing on the Shoulders of Giants!

As I look back on the long and proud history of hypnosis as a profession, there many brilliant individuals who have preceded us—the innovators whose insights, guidance, and techniques brought us to where we are today. Like all things in life, the evolution of ideas, methods and improvements need to take place so that progress will continue.

Forms of hypnotism go back as far as recorded history, from ancient Egypt and Greece, including forms of meditation practices from the East, spanning thousands of years. This entire profession owes a tremendous debt to both the innovators we know and have come to appreciate, as well as perhaps even thousands of others forever lost to recorded history.

In my view, to be rooted and stuck in the past with only a handful of approaches and techniques is to be trapped by the past, delivering limited results. It's time to upgrade and reach greater heights! Stagnation most always impedes progress and improvement.

Older Approaches and Time for an Upgrade

Older approaches, while perhaps familiar and comfortable to the practitioner, can be rooted in limitation. While the past has its profound place, there is so much more possible with our work. Isn't it time to bring newer insights and more powerful approaches forward into the world? For example, in the 1950s, the hypnosis profession saw a great many insightful and brilliant colleagues developing and creating approaches with clever and effective ideas, and many of these remain in use today. What will future generations of hypnotists think of us? Time to light the way to a more brilliant future.

My Challenge to You!

My challenge to any hypnotist colleagues or related professionals reading this book would be: What are each of us doing today to bring results to the next quantum level of impact and improvement? Isn't it time we began to professionally raise our beneficial impact and begin doing even more?

Much of our work is literally priceless, regardless of what we charge per session. One example might be getting a single parent or a single grandparent solely raising a child to forever quit smoking and perhaps extend their lives 15, 20 or 30 years. This life-improving change and health upgrade empowers them forever as they raise this child. When you think about it, this benefit is truly something beyond financial calculation!

Your Inspiration

And now, for a moment of your own professional inspiration. My best suggestion is: Right now, before going any further in your reading, completely open your mind to new possibilities, dissolving preconceived barriers. Be in a state of openness, while being a bit more aware of your own creative random thoughts, even if fleeting and fast. These rapidly coming and going insights are *best **jotted down*** for later review and development. Random thoughts often lead to major breakthroughs.

A personal example of this would be my work in *Speed Inductions*. Yes, they are useful not only in demonstrations, and as entertainment, but also for clinical session work. I have created over 50 speed inductions to date. So many ideas and inspirations just come to me I have come to understand these insights occur quickly, so jotting them down for later review and developing them usefully becomes a process, an opportunity best seized when available.

As you proceed, you will read and perhaps experience insights and suggestions impacting a wide variety of approaches, better and more inspired ways of thinking and ways of using these thoughts as new breakthrough techniques to help your clients.

I ask you as a reader *be mindful* of more fully opening your mind to a place more unlimited, while staying free of being trapped in any one approach.

Open your imagination, practicing forward thinking, mentally unlock the doors, break the mold, dissolve barriers—just open your mind. You never know when new ideas that can transform someone's life—even your own—might just flood into your inspired consciousness after reading.

Overview –

My goal is sharing my thoughts to elevate our wonderful profession to the next level, bringing forward many new ideas and powerful improvements, achieving greater impact. One effective method is taking time to think and allow your mind to wander onto a particular topic.

Once more proficiently practicing this, inspired insights, better ideas and extended thinking moves you toward better self-communication, a greater open mind and a more unlimited sense of empowered thinking and inspiration—which leads to more profound results in your work.

When applied to our work, your new and groundbreaking insights can and will more easily generate beneficial client breakthroughs. These can even generate an expanded sense of a client having more determination to achieve a greater sense of dynamic personal empowerment. Adapting beneficial changes and improvement in habits can literally redefine your client's life immeasurably. More unlimited ways of thinking will expand their thoughts and actions beyond past challenges, and even beyond limitations they once encountered as blockages. In this place of an ever-improving mind-set, your client now begins adaptively empowering themselves beyond blockage and limitation as a new way of thinking, while fluidly motivating new improvements, generating a more greatly inspired, self-adaptive capacity to rise above everything and anything they ever once found to be challenging, restrictive, blocking or limiting.

By better crafting suggestions adaptively, beneficially inspired internal self-communication arises as well as improved new ways of thinking, as a better as a sense of personal empowerment begins to transform their lives into a wonderfully greater place to live. As internal stories change, and lives improve, limitations and blockages tend to dissolve and release, generating relief from past restrictions, as active improvements more readily take place. Freedom and a more unlimited sense of thinking beyond blockages now becomes their everyday reality.

Hypnosis and suggestions can inspire and allow profoundly improved internal communication for long-lasting transformational change. A hypnotist can achieve these goals by improved suggestion construction and scripting. As suggestions are upgraded, we are in a position of helping our clients turn around most any past restrictions, blockages, thoughts, ideas, feelings, impressions, memories, habits, actions, reactions, and limiting foundational patterns which have kept them trapped. Improving internal communication via suggestion will invariably free clients of unhealthy habits and restrictions.

I read somewhere recently on Facebook, "Your past is only a story you are telling yourself, once you let go of the story, you are no longer trapped by it." I have often wondered if someone were to simply forget their past—including all of its traumas and limitations—and started anew, how much freer could they become?

When the client's subconscious mind is inspirationally directed to support and heroically take more optimal care of them, it can effectively become a powerful engine for transformation, working now in their favor to unbeatably yet adaptively set up a brand-new and better chapter of their lives.

In this new and expanded way of internalized self-support and self–thinking, truest empowerment is automatic. In this place of empowerment for every "I can't," there is both now and forever an "Of course I can!" For every "I haven't been able to," there's the possibility of unlimited improvement empowered by a true inner unstoppable hero.

What to Look For

In the course of this work you will find many new ways of thinking and suggesting. You will also find more insightful examples of suggestion writing so you can design better and more effective sessions, producing greater results.

The *ultimate object* is to create greater impact and more profound change, releasing unbeneficial, negative or limiting behavior and habits, while liberating your client's very best. We are activating their mighty inner hero to become a means of self-support, adaptively, automatically and consistently—so they can consistently create breakthroughs.

Within this new, better constructed and self–adapting chapter of life, your client remains improvement-driven, more instantly inspired, adaptively effective at overcoming obstacles, even heroic. Their subconscious is now released to work favorably; it's their new best friend and their functional ally. Their unbeatable subconscious mind, now always and forever working favorably, to improve, while awake, while asleep, and perhaps even while happy pleasant dreams guide the way to a better tomorrow. These pleasant happy dreams might just work out any sort of issues via adaptive suggestion and self-perpetuation, succeeding in ways both known and unknown to them. It is their now forever more empowered place to live.

After you process this information, I would one day enjoy receiving feedback such as, "This really helped my session work because I've reconstructed the way my session suggestions are written to get my clients where they need to go."

Sections –

This book will be grouped into several areas including sharing some personal life stories on how I arrived at this way of thinking, methods as an extension of life experience, and a re-orientation of techniques via insights and suggestions.

Insight –
What is your Intent?

Initially, I'd like to discuss a conversation I once had many years ago with my legendary, late great colleague, hypnotist Ormond McGill. He was my friend, at times my mentor, a genius, one of the finest people I've ever known. He had a quiet gentle way about him and an inspired mind.

Once, during a conversation, our discussion turned toward the concept of intent. Where are you before or as you begin, and where do you want to finally wind up? Where is your focus? What is your plan? And from one hundred percent of you, where is the focus of your will and desire, and what are you seeking to beneficially generate? In other words, what is your intent before

and as you begin any processing information to work up a hypnosis session?

Concept–

Personally, when I am doing a session intake, setting up, or
even hosting a clinical hypnosis session, or if I am about to be
performing one of my *speed inductions,* or even hosting a *Trance
Master* comedy hypnosis show—in fact, whenever I am doing
anything as a hypnotic professional, my core foundation and
functioning involves *focusing on my fullest possible intent to
generate, create and achieve maximum impact for the ultimate
result.*

This profound process is so much more than simply a wish,
or a passionate desire for beneficial success. It is instead a form
of focus from deep within the creative part of my mind, my complete will and focus from the essence of who I am, now precisely
and sharply focused to achieve optimal results. (Just as in the
same way each of us projects life force, or light out in front of
us to step into as we create our lives). It's like headlights on a car
shining light in front of us as we drive, and also how we drive
into that light as we proceed forward. It's as if our inner life force
light shines out in front of us from our essence, will and thoughts
to create the life we have, as you remain stepping forward into
that light. It is in a great many ways more fully opening our abilities to unleash our very best as to achieve ultimate success.

In these moments when I am working, in my focus I remain
completely and profoundly determined to generate higher
impact, exceptional results and perhaps instantaneous life
improvement to achieve a more beneficial ultimate outcome.

Giving less always will achieve less. Giving less is cheating yourself and your client, limiting one's results. As in martial arts, focusing your energy and your will in harmony, rising up in a mighty way to overwhelm, beyond limitation and shadow, in order to unlimit and shine bright. So too within your approach remaining actively greater than the situation at hand, to rise above and overwhelm the situation, achieving the greatest good and the most profound improvements, delivering truly powerful results.

Insight –

So some questions to ponder, some points I might ask you as a reader, to stop for just a moment to consider might be:

- What is your intent when you are doing anything in hypnosis?

- Where are you initially?

- Where do you want to wind up?

- How strong is your focus beyond any apparent challenges, blockages or limitations?

- How mighty and heroically inspired are you to succeed?

In your mind's eye, as if projecting yourself moments or minutes into the future, what does your result potentially look like when you get there?

Life Story –

Running track in high school, I ran faster in races when I mentally put myself across the finish line a short yet an appropriate amount of time into the future. I did this before the starter's pistol went off. During the race, my body would be working hard to achieve my desired results. In my mind, before I started I had achieved this outcome already.

It's more than simple visualization in this process. It's visualization, willpower, one's passionate desire to succeed, a focus of will, *complete intent,* almost as if you've already broken through before you have begun, truly beyond any doubt or shadow—a level of a knowing and glowing light of success. You have—in your mind and throughout your entire being—already succeeded before you have even begun. Success is your only outcome. Mentally projecting yourself into that success, as if stepping into success, will help you to not only achieve success but more regularly generate success and breakthroughs. For the greater the challenge, the mightier you will become when you are in this mind-set!

Let's say there's a clinical hypnosis session involving some kind of life improvement. What is your intent? How hard are you willing to work to achieve your complete intent of unlimited, high-impact results? How overwhelming. Can you rise to any challenges presented? Are you knowingly working to achieve improvement, effectively and adaptively generating better life-improving results? From the core of your essence, how directed and strong is your focus, willpower, desire and unstoppable drive for breakthrough success? Is it beyond even what the client wants or expects from the scheduled session?

For me, all I do hypnotically is at this level of focus, and my answer would be a resounding yes, I am there! I am more determined than any possible pre-existing resistance, and any resistance I encounter is more easily yet powerfully unstoppably overwhelmed. My focus and determination and my intent is unstoppably stronger than any possible standing blockage, like a tidal wave of inspired harmony and correction. Within my mind and throughout the core of who I am, I remain unstoppably determined to allow my intent to overwhelm and generate beneficial yet functionally adaptive improvements in whatever way is best, in ways the client can more effectively manifest.

Insight
What is Intent?

If I intend to move my body around in some way, I am moving my body because I am intending to do this either consciously or subconsciously. It goes way beyond trying and struggling, focused intent is beyond limitation. When one has this ability, it can more completely generate unbeatable success.

It might make sense at this point to discuss how each of us can project our understandings, abilities, talents, and the freedom each of us has, freed of restriction by a thought to manifest a different and better reality. Often that means rising above any challenge presented to a greater place of empowerment, activating one's mighty inner hero, focusing less on the tunnel but more at the light at the tunnel's end to unstoppably get there.

As a reader of this work, please stop for a few moments and think about *the idea of your intent* and how better to focus your intent more overwhelmingly and effectively to better generate impact and results.

Insight - Key Point
Permanent Life Transformation
Self-Perpetuating Suggestions

Writing self-perpetuating, self-adapting, ever-improving

suggestions is a critical component in our new way of looking at suggestion management and construction.

This takes place while asking the client's subconscious mind—most often while in deep trance—to begin to work this time and into forever, beneficially and adaptively functional within their favor, as an ally, relentlessly and unstoppably, while they are awake, while they are asleep, as even while happy, pleasant dreams give them a better night's rest while, more effectively now start guiding their way into a better tomorrow. To unbeatably, unstoppably and forever generate ever-increasing improvement, to support, renovate, upgrade, to release while generating adaptive forgiveness, to usher in a brand-new and better chapter of their lives. Their powerful subconscious mind is asked to work to make adjustments and upgrades as necessary as your client continues along with this new chapter of their lives. To self-perpetuate improvements and adjustments, to continually refine and adapt suggestions to maximum benefit, while continually releasing old habits and restrictions, while generating new and ever-improving health supporting thoughts, feelings, ideas, actions, reactions and habits, to make room for greater life fulfillment.

Their subconscious mind, often once an adversary, now a functional and adaptive ally, builds and constructs this masterpiece chapter in their lives. The perpetual subconscious generation of this masterpiece chapter of their lives is the ultimate goal of any client seeking improvement. This can be the *ultimate tool for permanent life-transformation.*

Generating self-perpetuation of suggestions, just effectively adapting drive forward success, is critical to a new way of taking your hypnotic success to the next level, with each and every client or group you work with.

Suggestion – 1
Self-Perpetuation

As you relax deeper and further, your now always working in your favor and now forever working on your side, automatic and dynamic subconscious mind begins to powerfully yet effortlessly, even unnoticeably, truly in your favor, work out any and all challenges and issues as they might ever arise automatically to your maximum benefit and effect, both relentlessly and unstoppably, while you are awake, while you are asleep, as even while happy, pleasant dreams guide you into resolution, release and freedom, yielding a better night's rest, while skillfully guiding your way into a better tomorrow and life, as you now know your transformation into a better chapter of life to be only actually true and functioning.

Suggestion - 2
Self-Perpetuation

Your mind now easily and powerfully generates any and all powerfully effective, self-supporting, effective, and achievable, progress-creating, sensations or feelings, pace or plan, thought, feeling, action, reaction, you right now or will ever need, to create adaptive and breakthrough success, evermore completely effective, in ways both known or unknown to you.

Insight –
Self-Perpetuating Success

Achieving one's success, as a breakthrough, allows continued self-perpetuation of success, which can be ever-improving within an entire life.

Suggestion -
Self-Perpetuating Success

Your always clever and dynamic adaptive mind is now working out beneficial ideas, methods, pathways, solutions, adaptations and improvements to generate success in these highly adaptive, yet effective ways. Most effectively and easily generating complete and ultimate success, in ways both known and unknown to you, and so it is, and so it remains, as therefore you succeed.

Insight –
Self-Perpetuating Resolve

Setting up the subconscious as a reconditioning tool to actively generate self-perpetuating resolve, overwhelming the past to get the job done will effectively allow adaptation around any potential blocking or restricting issues once found challenging, from wherever they might arise.

Suggestion -
Self-Perpetuating Resolve

Your automatic mind is now UNSTOPPABLY resolved, making up its mind truly and forever to remain just this way, [smoke free, cigarette-free – lighter, thinner, clear, better – etc.] in the morning and throughout the rest of the day into the night, each and every day, each and every night, driven to succeed.

Insight –
Overwhelming the Situation

When working my intent, whether in any private session, or

group session, in every demonstration of hypnosis, in every hypnosis stage show I perform, within any speed induction work that I do or demonstrate, is to do it bigger, better, more profoundly or perhaps quicker in some cases, than ever before, with breakthrough results and with highest, most precise, effectively useful impact.

My intent while suggesting life changing improvement is to overwhelm the past blockage situation, to generate a quantum rising above any restrictive moment, beyond any challenge, known or unknown, to the place where any challenging issue which needs to be to transitioned beyond is effectively taken to a place of easily being risen above, lessening the past moments of impact, as now all past issues are and remain self-resolving. In this place powerful beneficial results are achieved, adaptively, actively generating. (I know that is a convoluted sentence. My brain does that occasionally and it is a little covert hypnosis on you as a reader and thinker, because I also do that as well, and it may just well benefit you, at some future time, even surprisingly so).

Suggestion –
Overwhelming the Situation

In this place of inspiration and creative breakthrough success, your very best aspects mightily rise to the top, easily overwhelming any and all challenges or situations standing in the way of your progress and success.

Insight –
Inspiration - A Reorientation towards Empowerment

For example, when a person comes in to quit smoking, or

when a person comes in to lose weight, releasing the client's disposition toward problem orientation as a predilection, a habit, a sense or thought pattern, to instead do better, suggesting a subconscious disposition toward facing down challenges generates a better way of thinking and resolving.

In order to activate this, suggest they now develop a more driven and limitless ability to rise above any challenge or situation, to a place of greater and more effective, adaptive resolution, actively generating a foundation of fully functioning release, relief and the ability to transcend.

In this new point of personal power, the client is more easily able to step into the next chapter of their lives, creating their masterpiece life chapter, as habits, actions and even reactions, ever more self-supporting, more perfected and balanced. In this place better thoughts and inspired feelings arising, more self-supporting, effectively appropriate steps and measures taken, only to live better and more fulfilled, forever moving forward from past moments now inspired and empowered. In this empowerment, they remain, forever freed of backsliding, now relieving and releasing burdens, while feeling, sensing, even finding comfort, and knowing their place in a better life. Here new and better more appropriate inspirations, approaches, patterns, thoughts, feelings, ideas are now forever activated and in use, while remaining adaptively flexible and achievable.

Suggestion –
Inspiration - A Reorientation towards Empowerment

Feeling more, more unbeatable and now driven to ultimate and more self-perfecting success, your now fully functioning only-in-your-favor subconscious mind will and must now perpetually work out any and all details to support any and all goals you're seeking to achieve to your ultimate benefit, as new and better ways of thinking, feeling, living, responding, even existing in this brand-new and better chapter of your life are substantially reinforced on each and every heartbeat and breath.

Insight –
Release of Words and Language Pattern Blockage

Throughout the course of their lives and exposure to modern culture, many clients have adopted words and language patterns, which instill ways of thinking and thought patterns which limit their conceptional ideas and methods of self-communication, create limitation thinking, blocking from freedom and forward-thinking improvements, even restriction which hinders habit release.

In other words, if a client's thinking, language patterns and words will not allow forward movement into improvement past a certain point, it becomes necessary to free them by redefining conceptual terms to allow expansion beyond barriers into the next chapter of their lives.

One of the best ways I have ever found to do this is to suggest a change of their internal communication language from words and patterns of limitation, to words and patterns of unlimited empowerment. To break down most any barrier and to generate freedom, a change in internal self-communication terminology is necessary to generate improvement.

In fact, to a degree, this goes beyond mere words. These changes in terminology and in self-communication must be concepts which generate action into reality, well beyond any word's simple meaning.

Exercise -

For example, put one of your hands out in front of your face, about 1½ to 2 feet away from your nose, looking at your palm and fingers. First, think about closing and opening your hand several times, just think, take no action.

Next, actually open and close your hand several times. There are two levels of thought here.

There is the initial thought: close my hand, an idea, a thought, a concept which generates no motion. Then there is a second level. There is the thought: close my hand, which actually closes your hand.

On the second level of thought, movement and action actually occur, altering the actual state which your hand is shaped at that moment from open palm into a fist, then opened again. It is this second level of thought activating action into the reality around you. This level of thought is where your clients need to be to create improvement.

Suggestions in hypnosis need to be at this second level. Simply beyond words, beyond the surface and what they mean, but rather words, concepts and ideas which instead generate action with a change of reality. This second level of thought is where our suggestions are best placed.

Suggestion –
Release of Words and Language Pattern Blockage

As you enjoy deeper and deeper rest and relaxation here, you activate all the words, thoughts, ideas, concepts, and their adaptations, beyond whatever these words can simply mean, into greater levels of profound action and energy, to alter and improve, more easily and effectively bringing true improvement into your reality, to release, thrive, break through and succeed. Relaxed and comfortable, yet, completely driven to transform your life into your desired goals, a more self-perfecting place, simply effective and taking place, as you are and remain, happy, healthy, and safe, easily achieving any and all goals. For yourself within your life, this you now forever know.

Terminology Change –
Redefining Terms Subconsciously to Unlimit Potentials and Generate Change

At this point it would make sense to redefine various terms within the way people think to generate potentials and improvements, while relieving and removing limitations. Internal communication can be improved subconsciously, which will, in turn, inspire motivation. Transformation here is not only possible, but even more completely probable.

Insight –
Forgiveness via Better Self–Loving

More complete release of self-forgiveness of critical past self-judgments or once accepted judgments from others we assumed as truisms, and have since perceived as ingrained personal truth, will allow the ability of habit release and life improvement. While in hypnosis, I have found it critical to suggest a complete forgiveness of everything and anything involving limiting self-criticism, in ways both known and unknown to your client. By loving themselves better, they are in turn taking the best care of themselves and telling themselves a more empowering and better truth, self-lovingly.

Suggestion –
Forgiveness via Better Self–Loving

In this place of relaxation and complete empowerment, melting and dissolving away from you freely, are all self-restricting judgments, wherever they came from, as a new sense of freedom and personal truth allows you a more unlimited existence, adaptive and effective, forever succeeding here, as you now know and completely feel this as truth, as you undeniably and effectively succeed at all you desire to achieve, true maximum benefit, in ways both known and unknown to you.

Insight –
Three Ways to Wisdom

Time to share a couple of core concepts.

I have come to call these the Three Levels of Understanding or the Three Ways to Wisdom.

What is Wisdom?

As I personally define it within my own life, wisdom can be seen as a fusion, a harmony from a balance of heart and mind. Basically a better understanding and insight, a better way of living coupled with a better focused force of life energy, forever connected to a better way of loving and living your life.

As you find harmony between heart and mind you also achieve wisdom.

Three Gateways to Wisdom - Three Positive Levels of Understanding:

1. Belief

2. Faith

3. Knowing ← Least Effort, Greatest Strength

In my view there are **three levels** by which we think in order to shape our reality. Here's how these apply to clinical hypnosis sessions.

There is *belief,* a belief in which change can take place. Every client attending a session has belief to some greater or lesser extent. In any system of belief, doubt can always wander in.

Next, there is *faith,* in which the hypnotic process will work. An individual's faith in something can waiver at times, or even disappear, especially during a crisis.

Yet the greatest and most impacting of all would be what I call **knowing**.

Both belief and faith can take quite a bit of work focusing while on something. To believe or maintain faith in something requires continual and active energy and focus. This means giving what you have belief or faith in credibility, generating energy, and constantly providing more energy and focus to continue the process. Both belief and faith can be exhausting, and can waiver and weaken over time.

Yet, in a place of *knowing,* one has stepped out of the mindset of duality, wavering or failure. In a *place of knowing* resides no room for struggle but instead the client has powerfully stepped into a place of determined reshaping of reality to generate maximum benefit, because they already know.

It's much like when people call my office and say, "Oh I really believe in hypnosis." Or perhaps some others will mention, they "have faith their hypnosis session is going to work."

If I believe in some object like a water glass, I will have to focus a lot of attention on it to keep my belief going potentially. If I have faith in the water glass, I have to like keep focusing my faith and make sure it's there. Potentially one has to keep working at it, using both belief and faith to keep making it potentially stronger, better and redefined, as further understandings and appreciations are achieved.

Yet, if I simply just "know" it's there, does that require energy at all? No, because it's something I now know.

Suggestion –

From places deepest within, you simply are succeeding here and breaking through, this you now know.

Insight –
Crafting Suggestions
Knowing

When crafting suggestions for my sessions, my goal is to move the client beyond belief and beyond faith to a place where they now foundationally and truly forever *know*, once and for all, even forever that they are empowered and inspired, unstoppable in achieving their goals dynamically, even easily, yet effortlessly, and results just happen.

For example, in a smoking cessation session, the client now knows forever that they are smoke free, cigarette-free, both now and for the rest of their lives. In fact the more challenged they become, the easier it is to succeed and the happier they are about their own empowerment.

It is not enough that your the client creates and contentedly appreciates a smoke-free, cigarette-free life, it is more important *they now know it as unchangeable fact, a profound truth, a smoke-free, cigarette-free life is now theirs forever.* In this brand-new and better chapter of life, they only move forward in the true and foundational knowledge that cigarettes are released and finished, permanently and forever.

In a weight loss session, the client now *knows* that habits, smaller meal amounts, slowly consumed food continue filling them up sooner, completely satisfying them physically and emotionally, and perhaps exercise too are a now known and better lived way of life.

Although *knowing* on a conscious basis, day-to-day, moment to moment, as a real and profound truth, may be the hardest level to personally achieve while conscious thinking is taking place, within the subconscious knowing something is more easily assimilated and lived from, as *a new place of knowing* becomes something which foundationally changes and improves the individual's life and habits forever.

Having broken through in this way, the client is *unbeatable and heroically inspired* to become more unstoppable within all goals they seek to achieve. Activating your client's very best, they are inspired and more easily driven forward into all things leading into a better life. In a place of knowing, determination is unlimited, and more importantly breakthrough success is more likely. A reorientation of one's way of thinking will inspire new ways of generating breakthroughs and permanent benefit. The reset has taken place.

Suggestion –
Knowing

Already having broken through in this way you're unbeatable, unstoppable, undeniable and even heroically inspired, completely unstoppable achieving goals to generate breakthrough success. Your powerful and automatic mind, activating only your very best, inspired and more easily driven forward as all things active and unstoppably effective is leading you into a better life. Knowing all of this is a fact, a profound truth. Your determination is unlimited while achieving. Now *knowing* any and all of this, you are and remain reset, retuned, recalibrated, as better thoughts, inspirations and ideas open your mind to inspire everything and anything it takes to honestly succeed in generating breakthroughs as benefit here, your freeing reset has taken place.

Insight–
Their Ultimate Brand-new Chapter Begins –

In my many years hosting private and group sessions, most everyone is seeking the next and a very best chapter of their lives. This is an important suggestion to instill, as it lays the groundwork for unstoppable life improvement, and is the key reason for any client showing up for a hypnosis session. The ultimate brand-new chapter of your client's life is about to begin, approached with optimism, clarity, excitement and heroic determination. Every client wants a brand-new chapter of life to begin. Why not give them this suggestion?

Suggestion –
Their Ultimate Brand-new Chapter Begins –

As you relax deeper, barrier free, flowing ever-onward, your ultimate brand-new chapter of your life unstoppably begins, as you thrive and live here forever. In this place you are and you remain inspired while unstoppably improving your life, optimistic, clear, effective, adaptive determined heroically, and excited about improvement, most especially in relation to becoming and forever remaining . . . [Smoke-free, cigarette-free, lighter, thinner, healthier, better – etc.]

Insight –
Living & Thriving Now - Rather Than Simply Surviving

Another goal while crafting suggestions is getting your client beyond survival mode and struggle thinking into a better, more life-filled place, where they instead learn to absolutely live and thrive in this brand-new and better chapter of his or her life.

Suggestion –
Living & Thriving Now - Rather Than Simply Surviving

Rising above the past and all the struggles, now dissolving and forever done, you feel free. In this new inspired and empowered place, the past forever resolving, as you learn to live and thrive, creating better and only the very best, in better ways.

Terminology Change –
A Redefinition of Terms – Empowered Self Communication

It is crucial when writing and later delivering suggestions for your client's subconscious mind to actively embrace these new ideas created by better communication from improved concepts, via words and terminologies which will allow movement and improvement, beginning right now and into the future forever. A reorientation away from "stuck" words and "stuck" language patterns is essential when reorientation and redefinition is taking place in order to generate aspects of free-flowing, adaptive self-improvement.

Any word or concept which keeps an individual trapped in a behavior pattern is a "stuck" word or "stuck" language pattern. People have used a wide variety of limiting concepts, ideas, words, feelings and emotions remembered and re-experienced, negative thoughts, negative expressions, negative feelings, negative memories, reinforcements and reactions from the past, negative belief structures, and more to cleverly keep themselves trapped, keeping behavior enhanced, static or worsening.

For example, a smoker will tell you they need to smoke a cigarette in order to reduce stress and to give them a moment to pause. Their false assumption has become their now only way to have a moment of pause or to reduce stress is to have a cigarette.

Another example is reward or stress eating. Eating under stress leads to overeating. Having unregulated amounts of junk food after a stressful day is an example.

These kinds of maladaptive coping behaviors create a paradigm which continues to generate a continuation of self-destructive behavior patterns. To get someone to become "un-stuck," a redefinition of terms and ways of thinking become essential to motivating life improvement.

Suggestion –
Clearing Stress

As a new chapter of your life has now arisen, you release and relieve stress, automatically taking a moment to take a series of deep and slow and steadying breaths as your mind now generates a more relaxed and comfortable you, as any and all stress just seems to flow around you and far away, detaching from and relieving stress. Clearing, proper perspectives now arise, leaving you relaxed, and in complete relief.

The Nature of the Subconscious Mind

The subconscious mind has its own characteristics, ways of interpreting individual reality, and ways of learning, understanding and reacting. It is childlike in its perceptions, interpretations and understandings. The subconscious does not deal well with nor comprehend sarcasm, negative terminology and negative words. Instead the subconscious mind interprets most of what it perceives literally. For example, someone sarcastically remarking on their negative opinion of someone's hat might say, "I really like that hat," as the subconscious mind perceives that as a compliment.

Concept–
Subconscious Understanding

Some years back, bumper stickers on cars read, "Don't drive drunk." On the surface this seems a pretty sensible and viable message, until one understands an individual's subconscious, once having learned to drive the car, automatically and usually is driving in some form of "highway hypnosis," which might misinterpret the above phrase as, "Drive drunk." Now, thankfully, those bumper stickers have been changed to read, "Drive sober." Asking someone to "drive sober" means asking for what you do want rather than what you don't want. Suggest behavior you are seeking to improve.

In this way, it makes more sense to *ask for what you do want rather than what you don't want,* most especially when reshaping paradigms and crafting suggestions in order to increase life-improvement.

Avoiding Negative Words While Writing or Delivering Suggestions

When writing suggestions, continually strive for what you do want rather than what you don't want.

The same principle works rather well even in business negotiations and in personal relationships. Only suggest a better way, which creates improvement and extended benefits to all.

When I was first trained, many of the suggestion scripts I was originally given would suggest, "You do not smoke, you are not smoking anymore," etc.

After struggling with that idea for some period of time, many, many years ago, wracking my brain over rewriting these suggestions into a positive style, my question became: How do you get somebody to do something else rather than talking about what you don't want?

Insight–

When it became clear to me, I rewrote suggestions to read . . .

Suggestion –

You are smoke free, cigarette-free, nicotine free, breathing easier, staying healthier, feeling better, loving yourself and extending both your health and your life, not only for the people you love most in your life, but most especially, for yourself.

Technique –
Internal Thinking Reset/Reorientation –

Subconsciously Improving via Suggestion –

Melting Away Problems and Struggles

Your client may have struggled for many years with the issues they have come to you to release. Most smokers I have worked with have been smoking for decades, many overweight people I have seen have been overweight most of their lives, or have gotten even worse after a trauma. Many people struggling with sleeping issues have not slept well in years before arriving for a session. Most people who are overreacting to stress have been doing this for years. Many people experiencing a fear have been afraid for a long time. Melting away problems and dissolving struggles is key.

By its definition, what is a Problem?

Generally a problem is some kind of struggle an individual has been wrestling with (or giving their power away to personally, or even professionally) for a great many years. With the understanding that once an individual releases the struggle mentality and takes their power back from what they consider a problem, then now instead, they begin empowering themselves to rise above the problem. They are then deflating the problem, and now their so-called problem becomes negligible, a problem is now a *challenge* they rise up to meet.

Now Challenge Oriented - Problem Free, Struggle Free

The greater the "so-called" problem, quite often the greater the struggle.

I remember as a child getting as a toy at the end of a meal in a Chinese restaurant, a woven tube called a *Chinese Finger Trap*. For fun, you'd put an index finger into either side of this tube and the harder one struggled, the tighter the tube became. Most of the kids I knew growing up cheated and used other fingers to escape, but the lesson to learn from this toy was to relax your fingers and pull them out slowly and evenly, to avoid getting stuck. Quite a wonderful lesson!

Struggle is a lot like this, the harder one struggles, the worse it gets. Yet letting go of struggle while relaxing through a former barrier, and allowing time and inspiration to work, allows someone to persevere and succeed in getting loose.

When writing suggestions addressing the subconscious it is important to alleviate the idea of struggle, instead transforming what was struggle and reset it now into successfully motivated, free-flowing, forward movement, large strides, step-by-step, or if necessary, better self-loving, free of critical self-judgment, thought patterns oriented toward loving self-support, self-release, adaptive, capable breakthroughs, as for every step backwards, there can be now two steps forward.

Asking your client's subconscious mind to forgive and release problem and struggle thinking via ever improving reoriented subconscious self-communication, while moving onward into this brand-new and better chapter of their lives, into a place now more fully lived in, where reoriented thinking and self-communication is now become problem-free forever. They now live in this place, and as challenges arise they are consistently rising up to meet whatever comes. Challenge oriented, ready to take on and face down any and all challenges. Internal communication reoriented toward self-support improves as a new sense of empowerment rises up. This reorientation is necessary to create permanent and long-lasting change.

Releasing the subconscious concept of the problem and converting the problem concept into a challenge makes addressing the challenge and its transformation more probable and immediate, generating a sense of rising up to meet and overwhelm most any challenge.

Suggestion –
Challenge Oriented

In all moments of your life, most especially whenever challenged, your automatic and dynamic, your subconscious mind forever now always effectively functioning in your favor, has powerfully and forever forgiven, fully and forever released problem and struggle orientation. While moving onward into this brand-new and better chapter of your life, you are and you adaptively create inspiration, remaining both now and forever problem-free, and forever now and always, driven and a motivated heroic you, creating only your very best, while cleverly remaining challenge oriented, ready to face down any and all challenges, or perhaps instead, just simply creating permanent and long-lasting life improvement in ways most effective, adaptive, effective, and meaningful.

Insight –
Activating Struggle-Free, Problem-Free, Challenge Orientation Mindset

Another concept to generate subconsciously is freedom, moving beyond struggle and problem orientation.

Everything which was once considered a problem is now transitioned into a challenge, something risen up to meet and deal with. Challenge orientation is a place of new beginnings.

What is a problem by definition? It's a big monster outside the door that's going to bite your head off.

Yet, on the other hand, if someone were to draw a line in the sand with their foot and say "Cross the line," (perhaps this was some sort of childhood bully), and you stepped over the line, and you said, "Okay, now what?" then in that moment, what was a problem is a challenge now faced.

Personally being from Brooklyn, New York, USA, I tend not to back down from a challenge presented, as above. One can instead outsmart the challenging person who's daring you to cross that line.

So, in this moment of inspirational empowerment, transformation becomes more steadfast in your process when an individual becomes challenge oriented and problem free. I work crafting suggestions this way in my private sessions.

One of the points I make—during the session pre-talk when discussing technique and suggestion—is powerful, and I use it quite often.

I ask, "How would you like me to get rid of every problem you have?" Generally most people want to know more. "As long as you're willing to listen to what I'm about to say to you and follow through on it, I'm going to get rid of every problem you've ever had."

Now, every so often, I can get a slightly contrary person who says, "Well I think I would like to get rid of most of them." I'd like to still have a couple of problems, you know I'm crazy like that, I just enjoy having one or two in the closet somewhere, down in the basement, maybe in the garage, put a few problems over there for a future rainy day.

Once you get past that sort of banter, a Hypnotist can, via suggestion, reorient away from problem thinking because a problem is a roadblock. Problem thinking is the problem! A problem is a cartoon where they nailed the door shut with 50 boards and a bunch of nails.

Suggestion –
Problem-Free, Challenge Orientation

In this new and better moment of your life you're problem free, challenge oriented, easily rising up to meet any and all challenges, for the greater the challenge, the mightier you become.

Technique –
Breaking the Cycles -
Failure Free – Learning or Success

Some clients beat themselves up over past experiences, both consciously and subconsciously, recycling this pattern as they might remember some experience or as a reaction, keeping themselves locked into this pattern. If they had acquaintances or friends who inflicted these mental or emotional beatings externally, the same way they self-inflict, it's likely they'd run the other way once they noticed these people coming.

As you write and design suggestions, "failures" and so-called "mistakes" now become reoriented into *learning experiences.*

Suggestion – 1
Learning or Success

You may just be thinking to yourself, "In my life I am released and failure free, I either only learn or I succeed; all of my life is a learning experience."

Suggestion – 2
Learning or Success

You may even notice yourself perceiving or even knowing the following truth: "In this place of inspiration, in this brand-new chapter of my life where I now and forever live, I am forever failure-free; any and all things I once ever considered a mistake are now and forever a learning experience, working inside and doing better, for in this place I always learn or succeed. I embrace all learning to create my better life."

Insight –
What about failure issues? What about Stumbling? Challenge Resolution.

A key point to mention is a redefinition away from failure issues. In this chapter, your client will either succeed or learn something, as in this new place, only learning and success take place. Without stumbling occasionally, children would never learn how to walk nor run. The wisdom of a child is to fall down, then laugh, cry, or just say whoops, get up and keep going. It's important for the client to allow themselves this kind of resiliency.

Suggestion –
Challenge Resolution

Your improvement in this new chapter of your life is ongoing, in all moments, most especially whenever challenged, you now knowing better, choose to either learn or succeed, breaking through into only your very best, your best just keeps getting better and better. With every stumble or challenge, the greater your perseverance, strength, determination, as well as your ability to improve, learn and adaptively stay on track now forever grows.

Technique –
Personal Heroic Empowerment –Heroic Determination

Within each of us profoundly exists a true mighty inner hero waiting to climb out and take on the world. Defining yourself as less is a lie most have learned to tell ourselves.

Think about it for second. At any moment when people shined brightest, from an elderly, frail woman lifting a car off her grandchild, to a person in severe pain who had gotten themselves off the floor and out the door to a hospital, to a rescue worker who has pulled someone out of a burning building, there is a hero residing in each of us who was made in the moment of challenge, rose to the occasion, and has broken through in ways either great or small. In this truth lies power.

Suggestion –

Activating Their Mighty Inner Hero

Your mighty inner hero, the part of you that is powerful, unstoppable, doubtless, fearless, and forever truly mighty, is now breaking you through unbeatably into a brand-new and better chapter of your life, while you are awake, while you are asleep, even while happy, pleasant dreams work out and resolve any and all issues which ever once stood in your way, rising up unbeatably, you were doing better.

This heroic aspect of you is reversing back upon itself any and all now forgiven and released storm clouds of darkness from the past which now drift away like storm clouds passing by overhead. Instead and now forever even better, the inspirational sunshine of the better day, the soothing moonlight of a better night washes over your body, absorbing this energy and feelings, as you are reset and retuned to higher aspects, as a new sense of breakthrough determination now becomes your very own, in ways most effective and unbeatable. You now know this to be true, feeling it from deepest places as truth within, your truest and most foundational part of you, as you are now driven forward into your best, and into your ultimate breakthrough success, heroic forever, in the wisdom of achieving your goals, you are and you forever remain unbeatable, always achieving, completely effective, even undefeatable.

Insight –
From Limited to Unlimited – Barrier Free

For every limit your client once assumed to be real and true, when behavior change was attempted and failed, or worse, was never even attempted, now and instead, in this brand-new, better chapter, they are inspired to break through and become better, truly unstoppable. In this place, things once considered barriers are now dissolved.

Suggestion –
Barrier Free -- Free-Flowing Metaphor

Like a mighty river flowing down the side of the mountain in the spring, you flow over, around, beyond, though, any and all things once considered obstacles, unblocked and free-flowing. Now in this place, you adaptively remain forever barrier-free, getting brilliantly wherever it is you need to be. And like a boulder in this fast-running stream of water, any and all things which ever were once considered adversity, or ever once stood in your way, have now polished you, making you better, brighter, shinier, and anew, driven forward unbeatably to breakthrough success. So now and forever, you are ultimately successful, flowing forward unstoppably while achieving amazing success and goals, into this brand-new and ever-improving chapter of your life.

Insight –
Instant Change – Foundational Resetting

If there were some way to reach inside a client's mind to reset things, much like turning a switch off for an undesired behavior or instead to activate a better behavior, both client and hypnotist alike would jump at the chance. Here's how.

Suggestion –
Foundational Reset

In this brand-new chapter of your life, it's almost as if someone from deep, deep, deepest inside of you has reset a switch, a dial, a thermostat, or a computer of some kind, easily allowing improvement, refinement, redefinition, breakthrough, release and relief, breaking through, knowingly, as you unstoppably achieve any and all goals. Now knowing this to be true for you, your better reality, now lived, yours, realized.

Insight –
Unstoppable Inspiration

Another key point in reorientation is your client feeling a true and realistic sense of unstoppable inspiration. Unless someone is inspired to step forward and succeed, they rarely will. Once they feel a sense of true and active inspiration, they are now driven and heroically unstoppable.

Suggestion –
Unstoppable Inspiration

As you relax deeper and further, further and deeper, it's as if a new energy is around you, keeping you optimistic, clear, focused, and most of all, unstoppably inspired, driven forward, while achieving. You now are and forever remain heroically unstoppable, doing everything and anything it takes to honestly succeed in breaking through into the kind of a life you now know you deserve and unstoppably and unbeatably create.

Insight –
Contentment –

Change, for many people, can be unsettling. Although their *right now* might be uncomfortable, unhealthy, or even miserable, at least your client is somewhat used to living there. So many become used to living in the misery, living in a place they know, rather than transforming into something they're unsure of. When reorientation toward habit release is taking place, it's important to generate feelings and thoughts related to contentment, being comfortable and at ease, effectively, thriving within this well-deserved better chapter of their lives.

Suggestion –
Contentment –

As you relax barrier-free into this new chapter of your life, a sense of contentment and peace, living a better life warms your heart and your mind more completely, comforting. It is truly wonderful to be so relieved, to be so free.

Insight-
Strategic Intervention –

When a person attends a clinical session, my hypnotic intervention strategy involves having prepared my suggestions in advance. I request of them five short and simple sentences of weak spots via e-mail in advance so I can write suggestions reversing those weaknesses into strengths. My intent is to give suggestions so the client can overwhelm whatever it is or was standing in the way of maximum beneficial results. As a better constructed new chapter in their life is now unstoppably beginning, they become freed from the past, and doing dramatically better, and knowing from deepest recesses within that improvements are going to happen. From this process, their minds will automatically generate improvements to get them to where they need to be.

Suggestion –
Strategic Intervention

Your automatic mind is now working this out in your favor, always. Your best seems to always be rising, how easy this is becoming for you.

Everybody's Hypnotized to Some Degree Most of the Time

I have come to understand that most are in some form of hypnosis most of the time; living daily life or occupationally under stress, being overwhelmed even at home, maybe simply too much stress, too little sleep, or simply from being bored.

It is interesting how a hypnotic professional can use these naturally occurring hypnosis states, even when out in the world, at times to affect change, most especially in an emergency situation.

Life Story –
Crisis Intervention – Real Life Waking Hypnosis

Some years ago during one of the colder months, I was driving a client home after a session. This client had traveled by train. In Staten Island, New York City, where I work and live, there are four bridges to the island, and only one train line. Once in a while, a client will take the train to see me, so as a courtesy, I give them a ride back home after the session. It is just easier than having them travel on buses at weird hours of the night. One evening as I was giving someone a lift, I came upon a scene playing out in front of me. From a distance things didn't look quite correct; I could tell that something was completely off-kilter.

Have you ever noticed some situation, on a road perhaps, where suddenly everything was more than a bit out of place? On this particular evening as I got a little closer, it turned out a motorist had blown through a traffic light, causing a pretty severe traffic accident.

As I later found out, the driver was on about five or six illegal narcotics, and after causing one accident while exiting the highway, he attempted to leave the scene and blew through a red light, crashing into a family moving through a green light. The man causing the accident attempted to take off again, and he blew past several cars before pulling over.

As I approached this out-of-place scene, I saw a car pretty smashed-up with steam and perhaps smoke coming from under the hood, while a very pregnant woman was slowly climbing out the passenger car door, looking quite disoriented. Her also disoriented husband was behind the wheel with an injured knee, and their little girl—perhaps two years old—was in the backseat. All three were extremely shaken up, and the woman was crying.

There were a growing number of spectators, many who had pulled over to see this spectacle. But no one was doing anything to improve the crisis; there was no real intervention. As these spectators weren't helping, I was thinking for a second how much they seemed like some movie version of zombies—moving slowly, walking, gawking, completely ineffective. I quickly realized these spectators, along with the people who were injured by the accident, were in situational hypnosis. Their hypnosis naturally occurring as an escape from the harsh situation they just experienced. As I exited my car, I left my client sitting in the passenger seat, as she seemed totally oblivious, in her own hypnosis.

Being a hypnotist, and knowing something had to be done, I

decided to step beyond this group hypnotic state and do something. Someone had to. As a trained hypnosis professional reading this work, isn't intervention what we are all about?

As we are used to working with people in various forms of hypnosis, and as most people are in hypnosis at many points throughout the day to varying degrees, it seemed my intervention while rising above the challenge presented would ensure a better outcome for everyone.

Most emergency responders have regular training in how to intervene in this sort of situation, and I am not well trained. However, I did notice steam and perhaps smoke escaping from the hood of the semi-destroyed car, and it didn't seem to make much sense to me to leave the situation alone, as dangerous as it was.

So, I decided to focus on what I was doing and to completely let my intent overwhelm the calamity in front of me. So, with smoke and possibly fire erupting from this car, I stuck my head into the car.

After first asking them if they felt okay enough to move, while single-handedly pulling these people out of the car, I heard the woman saying, "I am eight months pregnant. I just had a car accident. And I'm pregnant, I am pregnant." As a quick reframe to take her out of that as she rose to her feet, I said, "I had nothing to do with your pregnancy," and she laughed. This seemed to instantly change her focus as she stepped into a better mental moment. Together she and I got a little girl out of the backseat.

The husband was stuck inside the car, and outside his door appeared another man wearing a red shirt. The two of us got the driver side door open and whisked him out of the car.

I made sure the car was turned off, then interacted with the man in the red shirt, who was in his own situational hypnosis. I asked him if he'd seen what happened and he told me the driver who caused the accident was five car lengths up the road. I *suggested* the run up there to take a picture of the license plate with his cell phone, then to call the police, as my phone was in my car about 100 yards away. "If I were you, I would run up and take a picture of the license plate in case he takes off." He said, "Yes I'll do it," and he ran and got the photo.

At the same time, with a crowd of onlookers, there was an older woman, about a generation older than I, who had since picked up the little girl and was holding her as she cried, talking her down with pleasant, consoling conversation and a little bit of song. This woman looked over toward me and asked, "Am I doing okay?" I said, "Yeah, you're doing great, just keep doing what you are doing." She smiled and continued along.

In asking the red-shirted man to call 911, my intent was to repair the situation and put it back into some kind of symmetry, to intervene beyond the situational trance-state most of the onlookers were in. Soon after the phone call, two youngish plain-clothes police officers appeared in an unmarked car, looking at me as if I had in fact taken charge of the situation. Getting out of their car, shouting in my direction, "What is going on over here?"

I replied, "That guy down the street hit these people. *I strongly suggest* one of you run up there and grab him." As if I were a commanding officer in the police department, one officer took off to find the man who'd caused all this. I have since wondered if they thought I was some sort of high-ranking police official, as it seemed pretty obvious due to circumstances I taking charge of this accident.

Now, being a hypnotist, you will get this joke. I've said that we don't give commands, right? We are giving suggestions. But the cops too seemed to be in some form of hypnosis. Looking at them, what did I see? Glassy eyes and relaxed faces.

Finally, a bunch of fire trucks and at least one ambulance shows up, so as the situation is now under control, I simply turned on my heel, went back to my car, made a U-turn and took a different route than usual and finished driving my client home.

As hypnotists, we are used to being in hypnosis ourselves as well as guiding people through the hypnotic process. It also means as experienced hypnotists, we do have an ability to step outside the hypnotic moment to direct things, seemingly as in this case, just as in a session, to an ultimately better conclusion.

Insight-
Concept – Time and Intent

Let me discuss here the concepts of *time and intent —intent and time*—as something quantifiable.

If I am doing a speed induction or even a private or group session, in my mind, I work on the same creative principle as Michelangelo. His point of view was that his magnificent statues were already embedded within the stone and he was simply taking away the portions of the stone that didn't need to be there, thereby liberating the statue from the stone.

In my mind, if I am doing a speed demonstration, my intent is focused upon the person about to be hypnotized already being hypnotized. I am just moving them moments forward in time, split seconds to a place from where they are already in hypnosis. And liberating them from seconds earlier into the hypnotic state in the present.

When hosting a private session, in my mind, is the client already hypnotized, but on some level and at some future moment in time, they have already achieved success, in fact, their success is unstoppable.

Suggestion –
Unstoppable Intent

In this moment in time, your intent to succeed is unstoppable, as if you've already achieved success, stepping into your future, making your future your own, right here in this present moment, yours, your breakthrough success, completely inevitable and truly unstoppable.

Insight-
Point of Power - Present Moment – No Time like the Present –

In the present, in this very moment, in this session, is your client's point of transformational power. Beginning now and for the rest of their lives, improvement, adaptation, expansion and learning begins, responsibility, drive, determination, dynamic breakthroughs, better more supportive thoughts, feelings, and proper actions to more completely reshape their lives into the very best chapter, beginning right now, and only getting better and better over time, on each and every breath and heartbeat, your client is doing only better and better. This needs to be the level of motivation and inspiration they are living from, your job as a hypnotist is to get them there!

Suggestion –
Point of Power - Present Moment

In this present moment activating, is your point of transformational power. You can almost feel it, relaxing now, you know it. For beginning right now for the rest of your life, more perfected and ever evolving, improvements, adaptation, and better life supporting wisdom begins, seizing responsibility, activating drive, in unstoppable determination, activating dynamic breakthroughs, as better more supportive thoughts and feelings now and forever thrive, to more completely reshape for the better, your life into your very best chapter. For beginning right now, and only getting better and better over time, on each and every breath and heartbeat, you are and you now completely reinforce and absolutely know, rising up to your very best, you are forever truly doing only better and better.

Insight-
My Mental Process – Success

When hosting a Speed Induction Demonstration or a Demonstration of Street Hypnosis, in my mind, before the hypnotic process begins, my goal is moving them forward, usually split seconds in time, into deep hypnosis and response to my beneficial suggestions. Within my mind, any session work that I do—private, group, or a demonstration—any show, from a place of knowing, mentally I have already succeeded before I begin.

Life Story –

Years ago running track in high school, even as early as age 13, I can recall mentally having run the race before I began physically putting myself across the finish line, while knowing that every ounce of my focus, thought, will and presence was already in some way both powerful and real, across the finish line, my mind working my body to maximum benefit to get the job done as smoothly, fast and as effectively as possible. The more a hypnotist is in this powerful mindset, the better both the work and results are likely to be.

One Life Story –

At a hypnosis conference some years ago, there was a woman speaking about suffering from back pain. She'd bought a used Jaguar with older and more uncomfortable seats.

At this conference there is a rule forbidding hallway hypnosis demonstrations. I decided to go elsewhere into a room to quickly hypnotize and release via suggestion the muscles of this woman's back.

I believe this was later in the day, on a Sunday, after the official end of the conference. Moving down the hallway toward what seemed to be an empty coatroom, I turned around to see some of the convention staff following me in. It was a small parade of people who wanted to see me work.

The woman I was planning on helping seemed really nervous about being hypnotized. She then told me no one had ever hypnotized her before, nor had anyone ever been able to, even though she was a hypnotist.

Even before entering that room, in my mind, within my intent, she was already in deep trance and receiving benefits, having a happy and relaxed set of melting back muscles, ready to receive suggestions and feel better. As she sat down, I explained what I was going to do, and within three or four seconds she was relaxing deeply in the chair and down in trance, as her back muscles unwound and the pain melted away.

Insight –
My Hypnotic Intent

So my hypnotic intent in this situation was (and as it remains in all of my work) to completely overwhelm any challenging situation. My hypnotic intent involves mentally projecting myself into the future where I have already succeeded in breaking through with the client, and in this way my intent creates an unstoppable force of success.

Insight -
Overwhelming vs. Being Overwhelmed

Let me explain this in terms of a monster movie as a metaphor. In anyone's life, in bad or challenging moments, and from a monster movie perspective, you can either be Godzilla or you can be Tokyo.

Most of us have been Tokyo too often throughout the course of our lives, haven't we? We have been wrecked, beat up, kicked around, even at times left feeling decimated. We have all seen and experienced our fair share of challenges and chaos.

I have had a lot of weird stuff happen in my life, just like you have. But when you realize whenever a client comes to see you, practically always, it is your client themselves who are pumping their energy and fire into the monster they have skillfully created. In their mind's eye, this clever monster is now hiding outside their door ready to get them, metaphorically speaking.

For any impactful change to take place, you as their hypnotist will aid in creating a paradigm shift. When you put the power dynamic back into your client, you are heroically motivating more limitless possibilities and guiding them to unleash their inner power, assisting them in generating this more perfected improved chapter where they find the skills and drive to now empower themselves, freeing themselves of past habits.

Reversing the dynamic empowers your client. Deflating these monsters is much like deflating a swimming pool float. When you let the air and energy out of their monster, you are helping their subconscious delete the negativity and blockages, releasing self-sabotage and resistance. Their subconscious now favorably unleashed, is once again free to generate more limitless possibilities, melt away barriers, empower and inspire heroic mightiness, release tremendous potentials and energies, overwhelming any unwanted habit, thought or feeling which once blocked their way.

In this place of empowered inspiration, this brand-new and better chapter of their lives begins, as they are no longer the overwhelmed. but rather now the overwhelming force, as their best possibilities activate functioning better, habit released and freedom in their favor.

It's almost as if all of a sudden your client will re-experience their own inner power and is now driven and inspired with better energy, wisdom, truth and knowledge, as they now are the empowered one.

Insight –
Your Hypnotic Intent

So now, to your intent. Your intent within a clinical hypnosis session might be to overwhelm whatever static or unfocused intent they are or once were coming from, which has been standing in their way. Or your intent might be to perform an induction, which is really fast. When the roadway called *the rest of their lives in this brand-new chapter* before them is cleared, your client is more easily empowered, inspired, and enabled to generate breakthrough results, often automatically through their inner power, as now more and always working favorably. Once intent is better focused and clarified, the client is more creatively, adaptively, and inspirationally empowered to rise above all challenges unbeatably.

Suggestion –
Overwhelming Challenges with Intent

A suggestion combination I had written many years ago is:

The greater the challenge, the mightier you become, as your automatic mind now works this out automatically and even unbeatably in your favor, while you are awake, while you are asleep, even while happy pleasant dreams guide your way into a better day, a better night, a better moment called your life, into the next best chapter of your life. Truly knowing this now, you live from this, for all of you is now realizing this and knowing this to be true.

Insight–
Their Unstoppable Brand-new Masterpiece Chapter

Another core concept in every session you host should be noted as having your client unstoppably begin *a brand-new chapter of their life*. A place where they are now and forever liberated, reset, re-tuned, re-calibrated, thriving and succeeding, their goals and the very best only getting better and better. They effectively move on from their past while releasing any and all of its imbalance and unpleasantness, into the masterpiece chapter of their life, beginning right now and into the future, for the rest of their lives.

Suggestion –
Brand-new Masterpiece Chapter

As you relax deeper and further, floating into deepest levels of relaxation, you unstoppably begin a brand-new chapter of your life. A place you now know you are now and forever liberated, reset, re-tuned, re-calibrated, only getting better and better. You have effectively moved from your now forgiven and released past while forever more completely releasing any and all imbalance and unpleasantness, into the masterpiece chapter of your life, beginning right now and into the future, for the rest of your life, as if any and all of this very best seems to be just happening on its own.

Technique – Permanence
Better Hypnotic Guidelines for Suggestion Writing

When many of us first trained as hypnotists, we were given a set of guidelines by which suggestions were to be written and shared. One initial concept I learned were suggestions needing to be framed in the **present tense.**

I always teach my students a *two-pronged approach* to this. Yes, suggestions are to be structured initially within the present tense or *right now*, and even **perhaps more importantly,** into the client's **future and forever.**

Suggestion -
Permanence

Beginning right now and for the rest of your life, you will find you, in fact begin and shall begin yet forever remain effective and free . . .

Insight –
Dissolving Limitations

Many of the these terms go into practically every session I design since my intent is to overwhelm whatever was or might have been reinforcements, resistances, blockages, and limitations, with a more focused and powerful intent which will unstoppably generate a greater, grander more life-empowering viable and truer intent getting your client's subconscious adaptively and forever to where it needs to be. Once there, living and thriving, in ways both known and unknown, as their subconscious mind is working this out for them, always by adapting, adjusting and refining.

Suggestion –
Dissolving Limitations

Feeling free and truly now knowing you are now free forever of past limitations, blockages, struggles, unpleasantness, any and all of it just washed away, evaporating, melted away, dissolving, released, even laughable. Completely now knowing you've moved so far forward, you just know you always create and will unstoppably yet adaptively generate a greater, grander more life-empowering improvement, getting you forever to where you need to be, in ways both known and unknown, as you are now functioning only in your favor, working heroically to your truest and most complete benefit, your automatic mind forever working this out for you, always adjusting and refining. Trusting in this fact, you now live from a better truth and knowledge, so much relieved, released and feeling wonderful, achieving all you seek.

NOTE – If necessary, please review the above to ensure you are getting this before proceeding further. If you are getting this, please continue.

Insight –
Harnessing your Intent to Achieve Success

So, let your intent in any session you write, set up or construct, or in any hypnosis demonstration which you perform, or if you do stage work, focus your session, demonstration or show intent, to allow yourself be bigger than anything you have ever done!

In each and every session, in each and every demo, in each and every show, this is my intent, my passion, my focus, even my will drives out from my mind into my reality, always and only my very best.

For example, from a movie, from the year 1970 called *Performance* starring Mick Jagger, there was a line from the film, "The only performance that makes it, that makes it all the way, is the one that achieves madness." [ww.IMDB.com] Now, I am not necessarily suggesting insanity, but I am suggesting intensity, each modern hypnotist wants to achieve better results and higher impact doing something grander, bigger, greater than any hypnotist before has ever done, transforming, transmuting, creating impact, inculcating powerful and profound change. - "Wow, inculcating, what a great word!"

Insight –
Your Unstoppable Intent

In anything challenging you are doing, let your unstoppable intent overwhelm every challenge, while being an engine of transformational change in the situation. This is a *key element* in the work I have covered so far.

Insight – Trance Depth –
Better Trance Depth = Better Results

I have found throughout my years of practice that trance depth is important and you may wish give it some consideration. In my hypnosis training even early on, most every hypnotist has heard of the six stage *Harry Arons Depth Scale*.

There are six stages or levels of trance depth in the *Arons Depth Testing Scale of Hypnosis*. They are:

Stage 1 - Light Stage of Trance - Relaxation – Can lock down eyelids, feeling lethargic.

Stage 2 – Light / Moderate State of Trance – Able to Lock Arm – Heavy Feeling - Catalepsy of Isolated Muscle Groups.

Stage 3 – Medium Level State of Trance – Number Block (aphasia), Change of Smells and Tastes, Rapport, Partial Amnesia.

Stage 4 – Analgesia, Response to Post Hypnotic Suggestions, Glove Analgesia (Skin/Hand Pinch), Partial Hallucinations, Automatic Movements.

Stage 5 – Somnambulistic – Positive Hallucinations (seeing something which isn't there), Visual and Auditory Posthypnotic Suggestions.

Stage 6 - Somnambulistic – Negative Hallucinations (not seeing something which is actually there).

[From - *The Master Course in Hypnotism*].

Insight –
Hypnosis and REM States -

What is a REM state? REM states involve rapid eye movement. Rapid eye movement, which is generally attributed to a shift in an individual's brain state, is most commonly noticed when a sleeping person is dreaming. If you have ever seen someone sleeping and watched their eyelids fluttering, or their eyeballs moving left and right behind their eyelids as they rested, you have witnessed a REM state.

Yet a Hypnotically Induced REM State, from a hypnotic practitioner's point of view, is when you start to notice someone's eyelids fluttering or eyeball movement from behind the eyelids, left and right while in hypnotic trance. This tends to be one of the better ways to tell whether or not your client is hypnotized. I seek to achieve this in every hypnotic session, demonstration or show. When an individual is in REM, they are most generally in deeper hypnosis.

Have you ever noticed when you have induced hypnosis, while continuing to deepen, and when you look over at their eyelids and you notice their eyelids are flickering up and down, and if you guide them in deeper—what happens? Their eyeballs start going back and forth and back shifting behind their eyelids.

My personal goal with anyone I hypnotize, and in any show,

demonstration and especially in every session, is to pay attention and keep myself alert for hypnotically induced REM states in an individual.

Hypnotically Induced REM States – Were They Really Hypnotized?

I've been asked, "How do you know they are really hypnotized?" The answer is I am looking for resulting REM states.

Generally, until now, most of us had not been trained to look for nor talk about REM states. To discuss REM states or understand REM states, as you read this, you might want to guess how many levels of REM exist.

REM states are similar to the *Arons' hypnotic depth scale*. There are six levels of REM, the same number.

Within the first three levels of REM, I have noticed eyelid flutter reflecting hypnotic depth stages one through three. What does that mean?

As my way of putting this, you are guiding them into a hypnotically-induced state where their subconscious imagination is more functionally open and working as if on the same level as a dream state.

When they are within the latter three stages, stages 4 through 6 of hypnotically induced REM, your hypnotic subject is going into hypnosis even deeper, and you may notice the hypnotized individual's eyeballs going back and forth behind their eyelids. I've noticed most hypnotists are not trained to know this nor think about working in this way.

When I hypnotize a client into their deepest levels of trance reflected by their *Rapid Eye Movement*, this is, for all intents, perhaps the best place to have them when reaching for high impact session results or hypnotic response.

From my experience, it's practically as if you put a USB jack into the side of their heads and everything you're saying is being consumed directly, each suggestion filed and stored, getting impact and meaning, as you are relaying information constructively for life improvement.

A science fiction metaphor might be similar to connecting computer cables into the head of an Android for an upload. Your suggestions and their meaning, and resulting adaptations are also being uploaded into the memory bank of the subconscious mind. These suggestions are directly plugged in as a new and modified source of power and life transformation.

Technique –
Deepening Trance States

Your task as a professional clinical hypnotist is to deepen the *trance state* to your client's deepest achievable point, opening their mind to suggestion, then instilling adaptive and self-perpetuating suggestions to generate improvement in ways known and unknown to them.

I have also found most people through conditioning are able to achieve deeper levels of trance as time goes on, through reinforcement. Some of the older texts have assumed the particular individuals only capable of certain levels of trance depth. My experience is quite different. Trance depth can vary from day to day and moment to moment. I've experienced this personally as a test subject in several hypnosis classes over the years where it was requested I volunteer for a demonstration. Most often I tend to be a deep trance subject, achieving stages five and six. Yet if rapport is damaged, my inner defenses keep me in lighter stages of hypnosis.

The more your client tends to reinforce their own hypnosis, generally with the deeper levels of trance, the more they are capable of achieving, and the better the results.

Insight –
Achieving Better Success

Your client can more easily achieve complete transformational change to quit smoking or lose weight, sleep better, reduce stress, do better in school, overcome a fear, survive a breakup or divorce, or anything else they come to achieve. This list also happens to be my top seven private clinical hypnosis sessions, based on my many years of practice.

Better success is generally achieved when your client is in the later stages of *Hypnotically Induced REM States*, which will generally assure more absolute and profound, effective and adaptive long-lasting change when utilizing proper and more effective techniques for greater session impact. Your intention is to guide your client into ever deepening trance-depth levels, for greater receptivity and suggestion adaptation to ensure maximum benefit in their transformational change.

As you work with your client clinically, it is sensible and important to notice trance depth level by getting a glimpse of eye-lid flutter or eyeball movement. Occasionally this can be a challenge, as sometimes the client might turn their head and it's just a little harder to notice their eyes. Sometimes there are low lighting issues in the room while working, or maybe someone has light eyelashes and it's harder to notice, most especially when they initially starting to go into a deeper trance. Other times I've encountered ladies wearing heavier mascara, which makes these kinds of observations a bit more visible and easy to notice. Once I actually notice eyelid flutter followed by eyeball movement behind the eyelids, then as I continue to work, in the back of my mind, I am smiling to myself and thinking, "Excellent, excellent" because I know something deep and beneficial is generally is going on, and I know what I'm suggesting is most likely creating higher impact and maximizing the effect to achieve greater personal results.

Insight –
Roller-Coastering – Variable Hypnotic Trance Depth

I've also noticed at times the tendency in some hypnotized clients to experience fluctuating states of trance depth while enjoying the improvement a hypnosis session will bring. Any sort of hypnotic trance is not necessarily a static state. People can actually fluctuate. For example, in my stage shows, trance depth in some fluctuates moment by moment. There are times when people look barely hypnotized all, and moments later, there in such a deep level of trance, perhaps stages 5 through 6. Trance depth state can also be variable in clinical hypnosis. Sometimes the client who was at first uncomfortable in the chair will later achieve a deeper level of trance, and as deepening guides them back into greater comfort and deeper levels.

An easy yet understandable way of my explaining *Variable Trance Depth States* in private sessions has been: There are three ways most people can experience hypnosis in private sessions.

Some people slip into a deep, restful hypnotic trance right away and stay there. These people are deep trance subjects.

There are some people, who, for various reasons, stay in a very light, practically almost "not hypnotized" state, and these are called light trance subjects. I have had many people in session who were light trance subjects, who, for example, had come in to quit smoking. Many of them had been smoking for many decades, sometimes three, four, five decades or more and many were heavy smokers, smoking three to five packs of cigarettes a day. Many of them refused to reinforce their session, as I always suggest, yet they quit smoking with me in one session. So yes, hypnosis can work even for people in a light trance state.

Then there are also people who seem to be a roller coaster, *roller–coastering*, at some point, in very deep levels of trance, and then they come up a bit, dropping down again to go back in even deeper. In some cases this can happen on and off throughout the entire session. They too also tend to achieve magnificent results in their sessions. I've also noticed this variable depth of individuals in my stage shows over the years. At some moment the individual seems to be in the deepest levels, other moments barely hypnotized it all, and then back down deeper again.

As I do not yet know what kind of a subject the person before me is going to be, it's important to explain the variance in hypnotic depth experience, and eliminate the client's second-guessing, as all can achieve beneficial results in breakthroughs, whatever their trance depth.

Recap –

In my view, when hypnotists are working with people, what we must be striving to achieve is guiding them into relaxation and trance to greatest depth, plugging directly into the capacity a **REM** state gives us, so that we can directly access and share beneficially constructed and self-adapting suggestions with the client's subconscious mind. And although hypnotic states can vary from person to person and fluctuate, in the long run it generally doesn't matter, as the subconscious mind will be working with the suggestions being delivered by the hypnotist. Personally, I never stop striving for maximum beneficial impact, carefully constructing suggestions for ultimate outcomes.

Creating Higher Impact in Sessions = Better Suggestion Construction for Better Results

Key Element Technique–
Self-Perpetuation

My discussion now turns to the concept of constructing, adapting and writing self-perpetuating, self-adapting, self-actualizing, fluid suggestions, which will, over time become stronger and better. Post-session, as the client's subconscious mind is guided to actively adapt, set up and continue to improve and refine session benefits, achieving long-term results through the use of more carefully constructed and designed suggestions. Suggestions should *never* be assumed as static.

So to now understand that which you're seeking to achieve, your goal is to communicate better and more profoundly once you've got your client into the realm of deepest trance and are connecting into the deepest recesses of their now, only functioning in their favor and self-supporting or ever-improving subconscious mind, which will now actively be working to complete the necessary expansion or transformation of thoughts, feelings and behaviors to achieve their desired goal, generating a brand-new and ever improving chapter of the individual's life.

Their now activated, powerful and always working in their favor to best possible desired results, subconscious mind is being carefully suggested to, while consistently refining, reformulating and improving their behaviors, life, actions, reactions, impulses and habits, to begin, for example, a brand-new smoke-free, cigarette-free chapter, or a lighter, thinner, healthier, better chapter, or greater motivated, or more free-flowing and precisely effective adaptability, activating drive and determination, etc..

Within this masterpiece chapter their mind is now wide open, ready to thrive where, for example, stress flows around them like a boulder in a fast running stream of water, polishing them, moving beyond them and far, far away from them, and into a better day, a better night, a better way, a better them. They feel this, they more fully live this, viably and tangibly, and as subconscious processes adapt and refine, knowingly living in this place forever, ever improving.

Key Element Technique
Subconscious Agreement
Now Knowing these Important Changes are Taking Place

So when crafting suggestions, why not bring your client to their best place of greatest strength, getting their subconscious mind to simply now truly know things have changed.

Seek agreement, via getting them to nod their head yes while in trance. It will be their subconscious mind agreeing to and approving of the change and improvement you are now guiding and, in cooperation, co-creating.

Key Element Technique
Achieving Maximum Benefit - Both Known and Unknown

When I was little, my mom and dad took me to church. There's a phrase in a prayer, as I remember it, "Heavenly Father, protect us from things both *known and unknown to us.*" Truly powerful transformative words.

Suggestions can be crafted to work *automatically in ways both known and unknown.* By suggesting this you are putting their subconscious mind to work on any and all issues, resolving and mopping up. I find suggesting the activation of success, breakthrough, and motivation, in ways *known and unknown,* generates unstoppable and perpetual, self-adapting improvement, motivation and clever breakthrough success.

Improvement in ways both *known and unknown* has truly become a regular staple of my session work, when I am seeking to create improvement in someone's life.

If the client's subconscious mind is effectively improving on a consistent basis, in ways known and unknown, then effort-free improvement is taking place, a key element in activating their inner power and their subconscious as their coach, motivator and best friend. The days of a reactive adversarial subconscious, now more than ever, are a thing of the past. What a relief.

Perpetual self-improvement is about your clients subconscious mind continually working out any and all parameters to generate breakthrough success, inspiration, motivation, new tastes, insights, ideas, actions, reactions, impulses, habits, desires and even determination, in ways known and unknown for unstoppable beneficial improvement.

Suggestion –
Maximum Benefit - Both Known and Unknown

To your maximum benefit, and in ways both known and unknown to you, your automatic subconscious mind is now on your side, fully inspired and unstoppably supporting you, while driven unbeatably, to your ultimate advantage and success, more easily achieving goals, generating unstoppable and complete beneficial breakthrough results.

Method –

As technique goes, I use this in practically every session I host, it also is a regular part of demonstrations I perform, and is contained within the empowerment suggestions at the end of my shows.

Suggestion –

In Ways Known and Unknown

You are unbeatably breaking through now in ways both known and unknown.

Technique –

Let's view and understand this from another perspective, maybe on a more physical or day-to-day level. My goal here is to get their subconscious mind to work on their side as a friend, a hero and unstoppable force, an unbeatable motivator.

A way to better understand this principle, as an example, would be the following:

There are a great many items in the engine compartment of

anyone's car. Most of these items are probably important, yet the vast majority of us haven't a clue as to what those things are and what purpose they serve.

But am I really glad they designed, built and installed these things, for whatever reason, to make the car run well and to protect us.

Consequently, when you are asking your client's subconscious mind to improve in ways known and unknown, the hypnotist is empowering the subconscious mind to reformat and rebuild the suggestions in ways that will generate breakthroughs unbeatably, automatically, and in self-perpetuation, forever adapting, more effectively adjusting to events, challenges and circumstances, while continually improving.

Story – "No muss, no fuss."

When I was growing up, there was a TV commercial with the catchphrase, "No muss, no fuss." A brilliant statement, "no muss, no fuss." A great way to share suggestions!

The suggestions being delivered this way are going to adapt and reformat themselves, and continue to modify and improve themselves over time, most especially each and every time your client reinforces their hypnosis through their self-hypnosis process, perhaps using an included recording the hypnotist has provided.

I have found writing, delivering and generating suggestions to adapt and improve, continually, in self-perpetuation, allows greater impacting breakthroughs while allowing and motivating your client to improve in ways known and unknown, generating a process of perpetual self-improvement.

Technique –
Self–Adaptation – Perpetual Effectiveness

In this way improvements continue to adapt and generate ever-increasing, greater success, while your client is awake, while asleep and even while restful, happy, pleasant dreams work out the release of any and all resistance, powerfully and easily dissolving all resistance, in ways known and unknown, to liberate maximum benefit and breakthrough. Potentially, each and every night sleeping deeper, easier, quicker, better, even falling back to sleep sooner, and to deeper rest. This approach also works well with people who need a better night's rest.

Even if your client might need to get up and use the bathroom or some noise may awaken them, they will tend to more easily fall back to sleep, slumber more restfully and deeply, with even greater benefit, awakening the following day more upbeat, motivated, and ready to take on all challenges while creating only better.

Setting up suggestions this way generally will allow their subconscious mind to automatically work everything out for them. The days of struggling and fighting now over, activating greater levels of their intent into action, as now success becomes theirs and they feel great. What a wonderful place to be!

Suggestion –
Self–Adaptation – Perpetual Effectiveness

As you continue to improve, any and all of this just gets better and easier, more substantial and effective, as time goes on. Your powerful and dynamic mind continues to adapt and generate ever-increasing, effective and self-adapting greater success, while you are awake, while you are asleep and resting, while happy, pleasant dreams release and dissolve any and all resistance, to your more ultimate maximum benefit, in ways both known and unknown to you. Each and every night, you are sleeping deeper, easier, quicker, better, even falling back to sleep sooner, achieving deeper rest.

In this more restful place at night, your mind works out to your benefit only your very best, more restfully and deeply, with even greater benefit, awakening the following day ready to take on all challenges while creating only better.

You may even notice yourself smiling as you realize the days of struggling from past chapters of your life, are now and forever released and over, as in this place you are only activating greater levels of smooth flowing effective action, success, and triumphant breakthroughs, more easily knowing, greater benefit and achievement, feeling wonderful, only getting better and better. Trusting in this, you are relaxed and feeling supported and succeeding.

Insight –
Inspiration and Optimism

I have found it extremely useful to give suggestions to instill a sense of inspiration and optimism. In a place of optimistic inspiration, individuals are more energetically actively motivated, unbeatably driven forward to success.

Suggestion –
Inspiration and Optimism

You may just find, in this your forever thriving, brand-new and better chapter of your life, better feelings suddenly are just simply emerging, even when least expected, almost like a weight has been lifted off you somehow, relief, leaving you feeling unstoppably inspired, and completely optimistic, now knowing better choices result in better outcomes, goal achievement is yours.

Insight –
Self Re-identification –
Liberating Their Inner Unbeatable Mighty Inner Hero

In your client's best and shiniest moments, in fact within all of our best and shiniest moments, each of us has proved greater than we imagined. All of us at some point have risen up to do better than we thought we were capable of, achieving something mighty. Maybe when it is necessary either for survival, yet always, in spite of any situation, we got the job done. This vital aspect of your client needs to be activated perpetually and working to generate powerful breakthroughs.

Suggestion –
Mighty Inner Hero

In this place of deep relaxation and inspiration, your mighty inner hero, the unbeatable breakthrough winner, who you are foundationally, and have always been, now rises to the surface in your life working precisely and in your favor, evermore completely, actively working in precise yet fluid measure, with skill and ease, sorting out and working out effectively, any and all issues, activating goals into your reality, as you now know this to be true.

Insight -
Inspiring Greatness

Inspiring your client to greatness will allow their greatness to come out to adjust and improve their lives. It is important to activate their greatness and all their best skills, talents and abilities to come to the surface and to work in their favor.

Suggestion -
Inspiring Greatness

As you relax deeper and further, as you now even experience, or just instead feel it, your inspirational inner serenity allows your best and greatest aspects, skills, talents, determination, and abilities to rise to the very top and work within your favor, ever more determine, and unstoppable in reaching your present goals, in fact achieving any goals you will ever need to accomplish, of course you can!

Insight -
Automatic Refining Improvement of Suggestions

As your client reinforces their hypnosis, motivating their subconscious mind to consistently refine, adjust and improve suggestions in a self-perpetuating mode while reinforcing these improvements, this leads to greater results!

Suggestion -
Automatic Refining Improvement of Suggestions

Your keen and focused subconscious mind is now improved and automatically refining, always, ever-generating better results.

Insight –
Empowerment – Removing Power Blockage Impediments –

A great many people have come to create over the course of their lives a disposition towards seeing themselves as "less." This can be damaging, self-destructive, and a power-blocker, as they stand in the way of their own successes and breakthroughs. These clients tend to shoot themselves in the foot as a matter of habit, working hard to actively and often subconsciously create a destiny of failure, while maintaining a low sense of personal empowerment.

Research has shown that the average person has 50,000 thoughts a day, 75% of which are negative. [*CNN* Factoid]

Of critical importance when working with a client is instilling via suggestion a new and more beneficial disposition by directing the subconscious mind to recognize an actual truth, that your client has always been empowered—even if your client has been in long-term denial. Now working with you, their days of denying the heroic empowerment within are now at an end, as truly, in this new chapter, their subconscious is now being actively reoriented toward embracing a higher and more empowering truth. Right here and right now, inspirational re-identification takes place.

They now are the powerful ones who by stepping forward, will and remain actively breaking and dissolving all blockages and impediments, whether mental or emotional, habit, actions, reactions, subconsciously now rising above any challenge, in ways both known or unknown, which ever once stood in their way, as the power within them is magnificent and now functionally active, refining and motivated, becoming an unstoppable force for life improvement, driven to greater breakthroughs and ease of life-long improvements.

Suggestion –
Empowerment – Removing Power Blockages

From this moment on, a new and rising sense of inner power is now seen, felt, experienced, noticed, known to exist within as you are embracing a higher and more empowering truth. All of you is now activating inspired feelings, which actively help unlimit you, powerfully driving you forward, onward, a better life, freedom, to only better and better, as a new functioning sense of a more empowered you is now more fully thriving, is now self-supporting, self-adapting, improving, actively generating all you wish. Right now your best modifying, rising up to the surface, in only the best, in every way, right now you are now ready to thrive, physically, mentally, emotionally and in ways both known and unknown to you, living barrier- free, as now both now and forever flow ever onward.

Insight –
Vanquishing Doubt

Someone years ago one said to me, "The devil is in the doubt." Within the process of self-doubting, most often all is doomed to shortfalls and stagnation. A doubter will naturally begin doubting the hypnotic process, it's transformative power, impact and effectiveness, and lean toward doubting suggestions, giving up and reinforcement, so that doubt can win the day. Doubting anything blocks forward movement, trust and positive personal transformation.

A client's mind is fertile to vanquishing doubt, even if old patterns that need clearing up are still present. In fact, this is why they have set up a session. It remains important to instill suggestions to adaptively create this pivotal moment of transformative power right now, undoubtedly better begins right now, a new and more self-perfecting chapter of their lives, paving new vistas of change, improvement, creative impact, while adaptively generating a trust in the process, while liberating improvements and transformation, truly anything critical to achieving a breakthrough and success. Therefore suggesting a new way of knowing and living, avoiding the use word doubt works to keep your client motivated and persevering toward their much-desired success.

Suggestion –
Vanquishing Doubt

In a greater healing harmony, your transition to a better life takes place, generating positive forward movement, trust, transformation, breakthrough, and success is now rising within you, a new and better way of knowing, and living, motivated while unstoppably persevering, generating ultimate success.

Insight –
Self–Forgiveness for Release Critical Self-Judgment

One factor that can keep a client stuck is harsh self-criticism. Many, many of us have a very high standards for ourselves, so high a standard, in some cases the standards seem to even border on abuse. Harsh self-criticism rarely generates any kind of improvement and prevalence is paradoxical, as it is negatively self-perpetuating, a trap locking one into old behaviors and stagnation. The fact is, if this kind of self-criticism were external-ized and the criticism was coming at us from others, we would probably be running in the other direction far away from the person expressing such a degree of criticism. Yet somehow, many people seem perpetually determined to continually self-criticize.

I have found suggesting the wisdom of a child can work wonders. Children learn how to walk at first by stumbling a bit, and when they fall they most generally either laugh, cry, say whoops, but have the innate knowledge to get up and continue doing their best to walk. Children have yet to learn the habit of harsh self-criticism and self-judgment. Yet some adults, for example, having to recover from an injury, in relearning how to walk would get upset and furious when they stumble, having lost the innate resiliency of a child. As a parent would generally be understanding of a child learning, so too, an adult must allow self-love to learn so success can take place. Every stumble is a learning experience to be gained from.

Suggestion –
Self–Forgiveness for Release Critical Self-Judgment

In this new a better place of empowerment, now knowing better and living better, you allow yourself the resiliency of learn-ing, rising above, releasing self-judgment and replacing it with wisdom, understanding, and self-love, effectively succeeding and moving forward in ways both known and unknown to you, flexibility, while remaining adaptive, guides your way to greater success, breakthrough, wisdom and understanding.

Insight –
Achieving Unity - Diffusing Duality
Success versus Failure Issues

When self-appraising, a great many people I have met and worked with tend to think in terms of duality, good versus bad, up versus down, day versus night, along with a long list of polarizing ways of analyzing the world around them and their lives. Life is rarely black and white. There are many gradations and shades in between. Yet, so many still continue with a black and white view of their lives and themselves. From this polarization, many negative feelings can arise, including feelings of frustration, guilt, and most especially failure, to name a few.

It is useful when suggesting improvements take place, important and even critical, to change your client's self-communication to a more inspired way of communicating internally. Seeing things differently will help them to reshape their lives, as new experiences become either success or learning. Reducing or eliminating the concept of failure and frustration reduces or illuminates blockage thinking. From here change is not only plausible, but very possible.

As life is interpreted from expanded mind, with fewer self-condemning and more self-supporting experiences and attempts to step forward, life becomes more about experiencing either learning or success.

And every time something is learned, it's now an opportunity to improve and succeed further, each experience is about taking strides forward. I would imagine the world would be a tremendously improved place if children were raised to think this way.

So in most every private session I host, I suggest this shift in thinking and in terminologies to generate life improvements. With fear of failure reduced or eliminated, harshness reduced and all experiences now seen as something to be gained and learned from, steps forward in personal improvement and transformation are now so much easier.

Suggestion –
Achieving Unity - Diffusing Duality
Success versus Failure Issues

In this brand-new and better chapter of your life, new ways of thinking and appreciating your life and yourself now seem to be arising in your mind, instilling a sense of strength, harmony, and peace, balance and flow, as you now view your life and yourself in a better way. Released and even laughable, the concept of failure, for in this new chapter of your life, all is either success or learning experience, in every moment, you improve, you gain, you win, you break through, even thrive and succeed.

Insight –
Fundamentally Transcending the Past

While constructing suggestions, another method to create a powerful transitional shift is to construct suggestions in order to transcend the moment of blockage to a place of higher wisdom, a greater good, a beneficial impact, and improved behavior. For in a higher place, in a higher wisdom, better begins and continues long lasting.

Suggestion –
Fundamentally Transcending the Past

In this place of inspiration you rise above any and all challenges, as things once considered blockage, so small, insignificant, so much lesser than you, having been learned from, you've moved on, rising up, brighter, better, shinier, newer, reset, retuned, recalibrated, absolutely thinking better, feeling better, living better, having risen up in a greater truth and a higher wisdom, your best and even better begins and continues long lasting.

Insight –
Activating Inner Wisdom

I have often thought there is an overlooked aspect within each of us which knows better and can do better. An inner knowing beyond disruptive life experiences, unpleasant feelings and uncomfortable, unhappy memories or other disharmonies are being kept locked up within us. This aspect needs to be released and be unleashed to activate our very best. This more powerful "us" contains higher levels of inner wisdom, inspiration and empowerment. And once this greater us is released, a better-functioning, and more resilient, unstoppable and more powerful person arises.

Suggestion –
Activating Inner Wisdom

In this place of higher wisdom and understanding you now reside. As this greater you is now released into the world around you, your very best now coming up to the surface, at your best, more resilient, cleverly adaptable and driven forward to freedom and success while even so much more achieving and unstoppable.

Key Element Technique -
Heroic Unbeatable Subconscious Mind –
Always Now and Forever, Working in Their Favor

One of the many key factors I find invaluable is to liberate and free up the client's subconscious mind. In this chapter of life, their subconscious is becoming their best friend, actively working as their true heroic liberator, functioning only to their very best, in their favor, freed forever of self-destructive ideas, habits, patterns, actions, reactions.

In this place, both now, always and forever, their subconscious mind is suggested to effectively transform, turning around unhealthy or unneeded life habits and reactions, while beginning to work out ideas, methods, habits, strategies, solutions and inspirations, actions and reactions, working in their favor, supporting client goals and motivation, which drove them to see you in the first place. Their reset subconscious mind, now focused, active, working in their favor, absolutely heroic and unbeatable.

Insight –
Gentleness Overcomes Strength

From the wisdom of the East, there is a phrase, "Gentleness overcomes strength."

There is a book known as *A Course in Miracles*, containing the phrase "Choosing to learn life's lessons in a more gentle way."

Many times I have found the following to be true, when someone is looking to institute changes, resistance might be from past moments of struggling and not getting any further ahead than they did the day before.

Suggestion –

In this place power, you now reside, as you now know transition becomes easy.

Insight –
Automatic Transition

This is why I suggest automatic yet powerful transition, in ways both known and unknown. Your client need not fight their way through improvement, feeling that struggle really works. In this new chapter, they simply relax into whatever it is they need to achieve. Once their subconscious mind has taken on the task of self-improvement, working on their side, very little will stand in its way, as long as release of the past and past self-judgments, and self-forgiveness has been activated, transition takes place.

Suggestion –
Automatic Transition

You know, somehow it just seems transition and change, in fact all improvements you have set out to unbeatably create, just seem to be taking place automatically and easily yet powerfully, on their own, almost as if someone from deep, deep inside of you has reset a switch, a dial, a thermostat, or a computer of some kind, as improvements so beneficial just seem to be happening on their own.

Insight –
Redefinition by Reorienting Internal Communication
Shining a Light – Eliminating Negativity and Doubt

In the past, your clients have defined terms and life experiences in their own negative way to block themselves. You can suggest new ways of internal communication and insight to generate new ways that are truly self-supporting. You will motivate and challenge your client to unblock themselves by forgiving and releasing the past to better and instead become mightier than any challenge ever presented to them. More easily right now they are surmounting all challenges. Because everything they've ever called a problem is turned around to become a challenge.

Throughout their past, they may have indoctrinated themselves within their own naturally occurring, day-to-day, self-hypnosis process before seeing you, these learned limiting lies to keep themselves trapped in some unhealthy habit or uncomfortable situation. Often this has been learned from others as a pattern, or has been generated as a way trapping themselves, creating feelings of powerlessness.

By arriving at your session, they've now opened the door to inculcate improvement in any way that's meaningful. So you, as a hypnotist, coach, or motivator, are there to guide and generate beneficial improvement.

Often we are their final option. Years back, I had a woman come in to see me to quit smoking. Her father was a famous surgeon in my county. She had tried everything to quit smoking, and she had failed, using a wide variety of different approaches from nicotine patches, prescription drugs, acupressure, acupuncture, auricular therapy, and others. I noticed after she left her session completely smoke-free, she had smoked and crushed out several cigarettes before entering the building, never a promising sign. Yet she quit in one session! Her father referred me dozens of patients afterwards.

My point, for so many people, is when all else fails, clients turn to hypnosis. And by working smarter, generating better suggestions and techniques, we create higher impact, and with all things being equal, most of us will generally guide them into breakthroughs, as long as they're ready.

Insight –
Activating Internal Power

A great many people are out of touch with the concept of personal internal power or inner strength, and have generated a victim mentality. Even more people deny this inner power, making victimhood a part of how they define themselves. By empowering a motivated client, by redefining self-communication concepts, by taking what once was considered weak and limited, and via suggestion motivating strength, the rationale of having choices and being more unlimited, transforming practically any self-destructive habit or response is not only possible but probable as limited belief systems are blown apart by a different way of thinking, living, and experiencing life!

When they come to more fully understand that all of these behaviors have taken place and have become habits, then they can understand that any habit can be altered or changed. If someone is capable of creating a habit, that someone is also powerful enough to create a shift, forgiving and releasing, choosing to do something better, in many cases extending their lives.

Suggestion –
Activating Internal Power

You already have within you all the drive, power, tools and techniques to change or improve anything in your life. Actively working in your favor, right now, and into the future forever, you set motivated into unstoppable action, everything evermore improving, as you have already set your mind to this. Your power within now demands improvement, and so passionately creates change, release, relief and improvement. Living within this point of power, at this pivotal moment in your life, in all moments of your life, your mind now creates revolutionary habit changes, easily and efficiently, in ways both known and unknown. You relax, trust and now know, you effectively accomplish this.

Insight –
Mighty Inner Hero Rising Up Unbeatably

A vital part of this work goes into empowering and inspiring their mighty inner hero to awaken and rise up unbeatably, to once and for all, freed from the past, automatically resolving, any and all issues, to break your client through into the next more perfected and improved chapter of their lives.

Heroically, let me ask you this, if one were to run into a burning building to save someone like a fireman, would that person not be considered a hero? Isn't there a mighty hero residing in each of us?

It's been said the hero is made in the moment. In each moment in the past where your client has stumbled and failed to succeed moving forward, somewhere inside of them resides a hero waiting and ready to break through, sometimes needing permission to come out into the world. Suggest strongly this is that time! Suggestion can tap into this aspect, a hero who is unstoppable, clever, adaptive, effective, driven, motivated, knows better, and always gets the job done. Unleash their inner hero, in spite of all things, and get out of their way as amazing breakthroughs happen.

Suggestion –
Mighty Inner Hero Rising

Your mighty inner hero, unstoppable, the foundational part of you who knows only strength, lives beyond doubt, remains fearless, courageous and mighty, has now and forever effectively been activated from deep, deep inside of you right now, powerfully and effectively, creatively and dynamically, completely effective and adaptive, who is right now unstoppably working in your favor to achieve your well-deserved and your very own ultimate success. The part of you who is fully capable of saving children from great danger, like life-threatening moments, is now actively working creatively and adaptively in your favor from deep, deep inside of you, to break you through right here and right now into a brand-new, freer and better chapter of your life, once and for all. All of the negative, habitual, stagnating and limiting energies that once ever blocked you in any way, or ever once stood in your way are now cleverly and affectively turned back upon themselves. Heroically, as you effectively and fluidly break through, here with ultimate unbeatable success unstoppably.

Insight –
Activating Inner Wisdom

In movies and literature, there is the archetype of some wise master giving sage advice or a magic elixir to an individual. Once the information or elixir is received, amazing transformations take place. As this archetype is familiar to most individuals, it is of use as a form of hypnotic suggestion.

Suggestion –
Activating Inner Wisdom

Within these moments right now, more boldly and creatively living within the masterpiece chapter where your now and forever better life begins, your mighty unbeatable inner hero is activated, as if given powerfully effective transformational skills by a wise master of your life, now at your disposal, effectively used. Reflexively knowing instantly what to do next, you always stay on track, bounce back, taking effective steps in effective measure. Completely effective, just doing so much better now.

Insight –
Vanquishing Fear

When you suggest a blocking fear is nothing, you are reducing the power of the fear as well as the power your client is giving to it. Empower your client to activate a new sense of inspirational heroic empowerment. As these suggestions are accepted, your client is now driven forward and releasing blockage, generating room for success. Fearful shadows from the past, vanquished by light.

Suggestion –
Vanquishing Fear

Any old fears were like shadows, in this new and brighter chapter of your life, the light of your life-force shines from within your heart and mind, washing away all shadows, dynamic and mighty, driven and more unbeatable, better and more unlimited choices, actions, habits, reactions, flourish mightily from inside of you. Your light shines bright, washing away all shadows.

Life Story –
Stepping Outside the Moment and Rising Above

Often in my life when I see something wrong going on, I have intervened. My philosophy has always been, if we are not all here to help one another, why are there so many of us here? As interventionists and hypnotists, we are as instruments for beneficial change.

Years ago while living in Williamsburg, Brooklyn, New York, I booked an outside session at a client's apartment in Manhattan for weight loss. To get there I had to take two different trains on the New York City subway. On the first train there was a man menacing three seated businesswomen, dressed in business suits, holding purses and briefcases. Their antagonist was leaning forward over them, singing incoherently, off-key toward their faces in an obvious attempt to terrorize and intimidate them.

In my upbringing, in bad situations, my mother would intervene. My father was a New York City police officer and I have many other officers in my family. I must have inherited some intervention genetics from my parents.

Seeing the situation, I distracted this man, drawing his attention away from the women. And as I exited the train, he followed me. The silly part of the situation was he was singing off–key loudly into my left ear, which doesn't work very well. As he's doing this, I'm laughing because he's singing into an ear that doesn't work well, as he's now trying to intimidate me and I can't really hear it. This attempt is literally falling on a deaf ear.

So he steps in front of me. He says, "What's the matter man, don't you like my singing?" I respond, "Not when it's meant to intimidate me, but especially because it's off-key."

He pulls out a gun, pointing it at my midsection. At this point, I get really quiet, focused and logical.

In this moment time slowed down around me, practically stopping.

His response is, "If you don't like my singing man you can go to hell."

If you ever had a similar crisis, there can be a moment where time just stops, everything stops. Everything around you just stops, you have somehow just stepped outside of time.

And in that moment, as things around me seem frozen in time, I see his body in front of me, and in my mind defensively, almost like a strike points on a martial arts strike chart, I see places to hit to defend myself, to save my life.

Now my thoughts are sped up somehow, yet beyond time, thinking, "What does he expect? What was he hoping to gain? What is he expecting me to do? Does he expect me to cower in fear because he is holding a gun on me? I should fight him for my life? Are one of us or both of us going to die? That I should get violent because that's my only response in his mind, that I should attack him back, or what are my best choices as far as he's concerned? Do I become what he wants me to be? How do I rise above this, gain a better overview and do something else? How do I not become what he wants me to be? Because as soon as I do become what he wants me to be, I lose, and possibly die."

A flash of insight hits, palpable energy. What is he not expecting? Almost like a voice from beyond, somehow, what goes through my head is, "Heal him!"

Time starts again, I respond to his "You can go to hell" question with, "If such a place exists." This response gets a reaction—this was the one response he hadn't counted on. And as I'm looking at him, it seems that his once overflowing rage is now short-circuiting in his head. His head is actually twitching from one side to the other, shoulder to shoulder, as he puts the gun away, tucking it into the waistband of his pants, and then zippers up his green army jacket, saying as he wanders away, "Does hell exist? I don't know if hell exists. I don't know," as he vanishes down some subway stairway.

So I change trains and I host the weight loss private session, almost completely unfazed. The client later contacts me to let me know she lost 40 pounds from our work that day.

I'm alive by stepping outside time, stepping outside the moment, rather than being swept up by the moment of challenge and succumbing to the situation, instead I go to a higher place, doing better than what the situation was trying to draw me into, rising above the presenting challenge, a healing rather than death.

Every so often, in a session or discussion, the ultimate threat scenario is someone pulling a gun.

So whenever I get the question, "What if somebody pulls a gun on you? How do you keep your power then?" I share within this story to let them know, not only is it possible to keep one's center of power balanced, but I've lived it. If I can succeed with a gun aimed at me, in most circumstances, so too can they.

Technique –
Stepping Outside the Moment

From a client perspective, whatever the challenge, suggest

they step outside the moment, go to a higher place, and choose to react in a way that instead better supports and achieves all goals.

Suggestion –
Stepping Outside the Moment

In each and every moment, whenever challenged, you choose to rise above, become mighty, heroic, inspired, even stepping aside from the moment to remember your empowerment, while performing all things necessary to achieve your goals precisely, effectively, easily, with skill, and grace from within. In this place, you live better, remain successful, with ever-increasing self-respect, for whatever the challenge, the more masterful you become, as you now always succeed.

Insight –
Time Travel – Like it Never Happened

If a difficult habit never began in the first place, then logically it would cease to exist. This can be a key inroad toward habit improvements and adopting lifelong better behaviors.

Suggestion –
Time Travel – Like it Never Happened

It's almost like you are jumping over the years back to a time when you were X (12) years old, and only this time, you are making powerful and forever commitment to yourself, so that even when you were X (13), you were, remained and forever where, (*smoke free, cigarette-free, . . . or . . . lighter, thinner, healthier, better, more active . . . or calm, balanced, rising above and beyond any and all stress, etc.),* for then, for now, forever and for always, living better, happier and more successfully in the very best and well deserved of ways.

Insight –
Traveling in Time Backward, as if These Issues Never Existed

What if your client never started smoking in the first place?

What if your client didn't spend their childhood being rewarded with desserts?

What if, from a young age, your client conditioned himself or herself to handle stress differently, while remaining calm in the face of adversity?

What if your client always slept well throughout the night?

Suggestion –
Time Travel Backward –Issues Never Existed

As you relax deeper and further, it's almost as if you were, for just a few moments, moving backward in time, seeing yourself at an earlier age, seeing yourself at the age of 14 (any age before the challenge behavior became a part of their lives). In that moment, at that moment, a completely pivotal point of power, you put your foot down and made a very strong decision, so certain, facing a choice, having made a better choice instead. So even when you were 12, 13, 14, 15, 16, 18, or 21, and beyond, it's almost as if you always were and you remained, [smoke-free cigarette-free; lighter, thinner, healthier, better; etc.]

Insight –
Traveling in Time Forward – Already Living in Future Success

Moving your client subconsciously forward in time, into a more true and profound place of knowing, as if now released old habits are replaced by improved habits, and goals have already been achieved, where potentially any and all challenges today have already been replaced by complete breakthroughs and successes. All issues, having already been dealt with and overcome, a place where truly these benefits already currently exist, as if they've existed, have existed, and comfortably and easily exist forever, as a matter of course in reality already for many years, generating breakthroughs and successes more easily and profoundly.

Suggestion –
Time Travel Forward –Issues Never Existed

It's almost while relaxing, as if within your heroic and unbeatable focus, with adaptive and strategic effect, all aspects here have been generating release, and forgiveness of the past, better behaviors and habits, as you have been achieving wisdom, to ultimate beneficial success, actually or almost like you have been (old habit free; smoke-free, cigarette-free) for 14, 16, 17 years, each and every day and night, as if you've succeeded all those years each and every day of freedom, (old habit, smoking) so far in the past, done, finished, even laughable.

Insight –
Issues Resolved into the Past

Each of us moves forward in time and lets go of things from the past. Those things, perhaps once important, currently are of little to no interest. It could be toys of our childhood now forgotten, a dance craze, an old relationship, since moved forward in time and away from, or any other wide variety of things now left behind, simply no longer of interest.

Suggestion –
Issues Resolved into the Past

It might really even seem like it's been at least 12 or 16 years since you last (*smoked a cigarette, overate, felt stressed, etc.*), it's just so long ago, so forever ago, so far away from you, so ever more completely far away from your mind, your emotions, your habits and your life right now. In amazingly powerful, highly effective and important ways, as you now know this, the benefit of release is yours as in this place, you are truly liberated, cleansed, and safe, yet forever free.

Insight –
Time Reinforcement

Suggest utilizing one's time more productively, generating improvements, and bringing up only the very best to influence release, and to instill the certainty of a better future free of old habits, as an opportunity to keep your client at their very best.

Suggestion –
Time Reinforcement

It has been said, the one thing we never get back in life is time. Every moment wasted on trivia, disharmony, imbalance and minutia, is a wasted moment of our most valuable asset, ourselves, our time, our life, and our life-force. In this ever better chapter, you are easily enjoying and employing all of your very best energies in each and every moment, to maximize every well-deserved, self-supporting and well feeling moment, thriving and doing your very best to seize each moment, truly making better every moment of your ever-improving life. Enjoying the very best of yourself and your life, better habits, behaviors now yours. In fact, every moment you are alive, your automatic mind now determined to live more fully, enjoyably and taking optimally better care.

Insight –
Mastery in Time- Flowing Improvement

If one were to assume your client 10, 15, 20 years down the road had already succeeded, and in that place were functioning with the skill of an individual master in the situation that is currently in front of you at this moment, what would the future then tell the present one? Unleash their inner master of improvement, allow improvement to become free-flowing, completely unrestricted, as if it's already happened.

Suggestion -
Mastery in Time- Flowing Improvement

You are taking any and all of this in stride, as a competent and skilled master of improvement of your life, easily and adaptively forever creating free-flowing improvement and success within most every aspect of your life. For the greater the challenge, the more effective, liberated, safe, strong and even mightier you truly become.

Insight –
The Dawn of a New Day – Challenge Resolution

Suggesting the client move into the dawn of the new day, in which all challenges have already been resolved, frees up beneficial change.

Suggestion –
The Dawn of a New Day – Challenge Resolution

Regardless of any and all past challenges, reset, you truly and foundationally know right now, in the long run, a better day will surely dawn. Just wonderfully, your better dawn begins right now, illuminating your life, evermore beneficial thoughts, mind, feelings, going on forever, freeing you and healing you, making your life the very best it can be, as you feel content and smile happily from, deep, deep inside.

Insight –
Activating Breath to Transform the Moment

Subconsciously manifested reactions can create difficult to improve habits. It's all-too-easy for your client to react without thinking, repeating old behaviors, practically as a knee-jerk reaction.

For example, if a smoker under stress reaches for cigarette, is likely the smoker will smoke most of the cigarette before realizing they've even lit a cigarette or had been smoking. For a weight loss client, after a long hard day, it's time for the reward of a dessert. There are a multitude of maladaptive coping behaviors people have learned over the years, an even wider variety of feelings, thoughts and responses to various stressing factors in their lives.

A suggestion I've given over the years which can interrupt the knee-jerk response to falling back into their old ways, involves suggesting taking slow and steady deep breaths, creating a moment of pause, a moment of stepping outside an old habit reinforcing reaction, to stop, think, to rise above, to do something else, something better, something freeing, and something old habit shattering while instilling a better way.

Transformation into a better way of living is easy, just as easy as taking a breath.

Suggestion – 1
Activating Breath to Transform the Moment

As you relax, from now on, focusing on your freedom, your inspiration, and you now know you are living forever within this brand-new and better functioning, living chapter of your life, in any moment, most especially whenever challenged in any way, you may immediately find, somehow, before reacting in an old way, you always now take one slow and steady deep breath, hold it for a moment, releasing it very slowly, and as this happens, a mental shift toward the higher, an inspirational shift in consciousness knowingly is felt and takes place, stepping outside the old moment into a new moment, you are. And in this moment you think, reflect, and decide to do something better. Being true to yourself, responding better, how great it is to feel and be so

free! Forever now, your supportive automatic and self-perpetuating improvements are taking place, it's just as easy as taking a
breath, improving always on each and every breath you take.

Suggestion – 2
Activating Breath to Transform the Moment

In this brand-new and better chapter of your life, your correct response to any and all challenges or stress is to relax by deep
breathing, slow and steady breath, your way right through any
and all feelings and actions, which ever once stood in your way.
You are feeling, and healing, doing simply better.

Insight –
Working in Compassion Rather than Sympathy

It is also important when you work, that perspective remains
objective by staying in a place of compassion rather than a place
of sympathy. Compassion is a balance of heart and mind, a loving wisdom, a harmony within which allows higher healing
transformation to take place—remaining effective to balance
challenges rather than being swept up.

In my view, sympathy is limited, lower, destroys objectivity
while it assumes an egotistical point of view. In sympathy, an
assumption is often made that the client is in much worse shape
than the person helping them. Forms of pity can enter in.

Sympathy leads to limited thinking patterns, destroying
objectivity. Thoughts like, "Better I take in their energy, pull negativity out of them and put into me." When this form of transfer-
ence takes place, objectivity is impossible, and the hypnotist has
completely lost perspective, becoming relatively useless, while
entering into a state of disharmony, much like the client they are

seeking to help.

When a hypnotist approaches a session from a place of compassion rather than sympathy, only then is true transformation possible. I have met some colleagues over the years, who, through feelings of sympathy, absorb lower level energy and somehow become more like their clients. This comes from not working from a more whole and unified place of healing and harmony known as compassion.

To stay in objective compassion, in your mind it becomes necessary to step outside the client's moment and emotions, to remain focused on driving forward achievable goals.

If you're a parent, potentially you are taller than your children when they are little. With that difference in height, you had an overview of what was going on and more effectively remained free of being swept up in the moment. If the child is having a tantrum, it's rare to see a parent simultaneously also rolling around on the floor breaking into a tantrum next to the child rolling around on the floor. A higher perspective and objectivity are maintained.

When I teach this concept of compassion versus sympathy, I discuss the idea of putting one's hands near a flame to see how hot the fire is without putting one's hand actually into the flame. Putting one's hand into the flame is sympathy, putting one's hand near the flame to feel the heat, maintaining safety and objectivity, is compassion. Submerging oneself in someone else's imbalanced emotional state destroys objectivity and shatters one's ability to intervene successfully.

To remain free of getting burned by various client emotional states, remain in compassion to stay effective. You can remain objective as long as you remain free of getting swept up by presenting emotions which can arise.

Insight –
Activating Higher Perspectives

So the idea here is to come from a point of view of higher perspective so as an intervening hypnotist, you can more compassionately step aside from the moment and throughout all those moments and remain objective, keep perspectives, and become a motivating factor for positive transformational change through hypnotic suggestion.

Suggestion –
Activating Higher Perspectives

Right now and forever more easily and adaptively, effectively and powerfully, you dynamically rise above any and all situations and challenges presenting themselves, both great and small, keeping distance to safely overview to succeed, becoming your own great heroic innovator, instituting well-deserved and beneficial change in your life.

Insight –
Insight – Living It

You might be wondering long about now, how did I come to all of this? I have spent a decade doing private session work, and I have given much thought about many things that have occurred in my life and the lives of the people around me. But when I am at my best, I do my best to really live these ideas and concepts. And from writing suggestions and reviewing aspects within my own life in the world around me, much of these insights have developed as not only a way of helping other people, but also doing my best to live them in my own life.

Life Story –
Rising Above the Moment - Saving Lives

Here is another time that thinking this way and stepping outside the moment also saved my life.

Years back, after the loss of a family member and just after one of my birthdays ending in a zero, while I was at the Jersey shore for a weekend with some friends, I decided it was time to something completely wild.

I was in the beach town of Belmar when I decided, along with a couple of people I had just met (a couple of ladies and another guy who was a friend of a friend) to go swimming at about 1:00 am.

At this hour the beach is very poorly lit. The nearest lights are further inland, and from the boardwalk it's about a quarter of a mile or so from the shoreline back to civilization. So we jumped into the water and start swimming around, splashing and having a great time.

Soon with the waves and currents, it being a very dark night, everyone lost their perspective of where things were, and suddenly the three people I was with began to panic, not knowing which way to climb out of the ocean. For a second or so I felt their fear, but also very strongly, I knew buying into and surrendering to fear would likely drown every one of us.

The three began to panic while I remained calm, stepping outside the moment. One of the women looked at me and yelled, "We're going to die, going to drown!" I just smiled and started laughing. This response seemed to generate anger.

Another of the women said, "Aren't you afraid you're going to die?" I told her no, I wasn't afraid to die, but as far as I knew no one was going to die that night.

Panicking, she responded, "Do you know where the shore is?"

Telling the truth, I replied, "No I don't."

"Then we're all going to die!"

Remaining calm while rising above the ensuing panic around me, and to calm things down, I said, "Just wait a minute, while I don't know where this shore is, if I remain calm, I can reason out where it is."

"What?"

I said, "I can reason out where the shore is. Calm down and just listen to me, no one is going to die."

"What?" she said, as she was still panicking.

"Take some slow and steady deep breaths, calm down for a minute and just listen. Which way are the waves rolling? Toward the sand on the shoreline or out toward the ocean?"

"Towards the sand on the beach," she replied.

"Therefore if we swim with the waves slapping the back of our heads, I would imagine we are likely to find land pretty quickly."

We did just that, got onto the sand, sat for a bit and calmed down. Crisis over.

My point in sharing this story is relating a personal example of stepping outside the moment, refocusing one's energies, remaining better focused to achieve the clarity empowerment brings, to immediately rise above a crisis situation, stay safe, while becoming unstoppable in achieving success as a goal. To do less would have meant death.

This same mode of thinking can be suggested to your client when setting up life-supporting new habits. Rather than responding in a knee-jerk reaction to stress and lighting up a cigarette for example, you can suggest your client's subconscious mind reacts differently by responding to stress and now reacting by taking one slow and steadying deep breath, allowing for a mental shift of realization, clarity, strongly focused on making a better choice.

Suggestion –
Rising Above the Moment

In this brand-new chapter of your life, most especially whenever stressed or challenged, you will likely find yourself instead responding by taking slow and steadying deep breaths, as a mental shift occurs taking you outside and above the moment, generating a new awareness, while now making a better choice, very cleverly and adaptively becoming, forever remaining (smoke-free cigarette-free) while enjoying soothing relaxation breath calming you down, creating your empowerment shift, feeling it, even knowing it.

Insight –
Taking Back Power

This same approach can be suggested when empowering your clients. All too often your clients are used to surrendering their power to situations, circumstances, old memories and feelings, even people, rather than empowering themselves.

Suggestion –
Taking Back Power

In any moment whenever challenged, you stop, deep breathe, relax, and immediately feel a relaxation power shift in your favor. In that pivotal moment, you become so inspired to step outside the moment, slow, and feel steady soothing breath, and inspired greater wisdom, understanding and truth now upon you, more perfectly reconfiguring, while knowing and truly inspired, heroic, enabled to succeed, relaxed and enabled to rise above, to be mighty, and choose to do something better, self-respectful and self-loving always.

Insight –
Sparking the Subconscious to do Improvement Work Via Imagination - "Just Imagine"

Once you realize the more unlimited potentials and power of an individual's subconscious mind and the subconscious can be guided for perpetual self-improvement, the possibilities of harnessing such limitless empowerment are potentially endless.

For so many years, various beliefs have generated conditioning, instilled by internal and external reinforcement. So your client's subconscious mind has been often conditioned to be working in an adversarial way.

Better, self-adapting, self-perpetuating suggestion allows us to guide the subconscious mind to become inspired, heroic, to generate surprisingly effective yet skillful adaptations to enhance your client's life automatically.

Insight –
Imagination – Thought – Plan – Action

And just as most anyone can imagine a greater improvement, this powerful way to suggest their imagination set up a better future, better habits, better motivation and more carefully laid-out ideas become plans, eventually activating those plans into a better reality and life for your client.

From this place, all internal conflicts are slowly simmering down. From this place, old habits, hindrances, barriers, blockages are now dissolving, resolving, and releasing, generating freedom, better thinking, better choices, better behavior, a better and healthier life in general.

For anything in the world to take shape first it must be imagined. In order to get dressed in the morning, one has to have the imagination to know how to get dressed. Throughout history, in order to build anything, imagination had to be used.

Sparking your client's imagination generates automatic improvement coupled with a sense of benefit with better rewards, which is also a key element in achieving personal goals. Suggesting the subconscious mind is laying the groundwork for greater potentials through imagination, in ways believable and achievable, yields results.

Suggestion –
"Just Imagine"

As you relax deeper and further into this better, well-deserved and more appropriately fulfilling chapter of your life, just imagine how great you are at more easily and effectively resolving challenges. Rising above any and all challenges, and settling into relaxing while remaining in proper perspective, motivated, even dynamically driven, to achieve any and all goals. Just imagine how great it feels, just imagine how easier it's becoming each and every day and night, just getting better at it. Just imagine how your imagination is now working unbeatably in your favor to generate only your very best, in ways beneficial to yourself and your life. New ways, better ways.

Insight –
As If

Another phrase I use in suggestion construction sparking the imagination is use of the phrase, *as if.*

Without your clients' ability to imagine better, rarely will success be smooth running. *As if* they are forever smoke-free cigarette-free; *as if* they are lighter, thinner, healthier, better; *as if* they are reacting to the world around them in a more comfortable and stress-free way; *as if* each and every night at bedtime, all daily activities and cares are put up on a shelf, as that day is taking care of itself; *as if* they have grown up a few years into the future, and things that have recently found challenging, seem so many years ago and so much less important. The phrase *as if* sparks imagination and action just as if changes have already taken place.

Suggestion – 1
As If

As if 10, 16, 17 years further down the road, *as if* someone, somehow automatically, all aspects of this improvement are happening on their own, *as if* barriers once there have melted away, *as if* a mighty river flowing down the side of the mountain in the spring is moving you around, through, over and beyond, to wherever it is you need to finally be on this, living and knowing ultimate success.

Suggestion – 2
As If

It's *as if* all and any old ways have simply evaporated *as if* the old ways have evaporated.

Suggestion – 3
As If

It's *as if* the clouds from the storm once there had drifted away, while right now bright and wonderful Golden-white sunshine, were shimmering, or at night, *as if* iridescent moonlight embraces and inspires you with a can-do energy, or even *as if* white puffy-fluffy clouds have serenely and happily filled into a better space inspiring success while fulfilling and supporting you.

Suggestion – 4
As If

As if old issues have been completely forgiven and perhaps instead released, resolved, moved forward from just *as if* so many decades ago and glowing bright in your mind, truly *as if* glowing in the inside and the outside feeling wonderful. I wonder if you have even yet realized . . . Imagining the life you lead *as if* free of this now and forever.

Suggestion Starters/Reinforcers –

As if . . .as if guided from on high, even blessed

As if . . .driven forward, you are unbeatable

As if . . .now knowing this

As if . . .with the skill of an ancient master knowing better, you're doing better

As if . . . ten, sixteen, seventeen years further down the road

As if . . . somehow all of this is somehow *automatically* happening on its own

As if . . . barriers once there, have now melted away forever

As if . . . you are as a mighty river flowing down the side of the mountain in the spring, around, over, though, and beyond to where ever you forever need to be.

As if . . . the old ways have simply evaporated

As if . . . the clouds of the storm once there, have drifted away, far away, sunshine, moonlight, all white, puffy, fluffy clouds have filled in that space, fulfilling and supporting breakthroughs and success.

As if . . . all issues have been completely forgiven or perhaps instead released, resolved, and moved forward far away from, so many decades ago

Almost like . . . you are glowing in heart and mind, glowing on the inside and the outside, feeling wonderful

I wonder if you even yet realize . . .

Just Imagine a now better life you lead . . .

Suggestion –
Almost As If

Almost as if having completely resolved any and all issues, and dissolved them away forever in ways known and unknown.

Your mind is automatically self-reinforcing to maximum benefit any and all of this.

Insight –
What If

What if all issues and habits now releasing, resolved on their own?

Suggestion –
What If

As you relax, *what if* the possibilities of freedom and complete old habit resolution are simply now yours? *What if* this has already been taken care of and now done?

Insight –
An Assumed Premise as Truth

When I was in college I studied philosophical logic, a subject I found really worth studying. I find it interesting how much of those insights I learned have stayed with me for so long. I quite often have noticed illogical arguments presented during political speeches to further some particular politician's political agenda. Many of those speeches appeal to emotion and pity or assume a particular premise as a truth.

Yet, when suggesting improvement to the subconscious in order to release old habits and to generate beneficial improvements, having the subconscious assuming a new truth can be a powerful tool for goal achievement. So, an additional language pattern that works well is: *You will find* or *maybe you will just notice*. Obviously an assumed truth, but nonetheless a powerful tool. As the subconscious mind interprets things literally, and not always logically, this is an extremely useful method of suggestion.

Suggestion –
An Assumed Premise as Truth

In this brand-new beginning of your life, you will find or maybe even better instead, you will just simply notice all improvements happening all around you, as if this is the way it has been your whole life, or instead, just so many years, the place where you currently live.

Suggestion –
You Will Find

You will find all of this taking place, automatically to maximum benefit.

Suggestion –
You'll Just Notice

Someday maybe you'll just notice yourself living the life you've always dreamed of, (forever smoke-free cigarette-free; feeling wonderful, lighter, thinner, healthier, better; etc.).

Insight –
Improvement as a New and More Complete Destiny

What if the subconscious mind were to embrace the concept of improvement about to take place as a source of destiny, just as if there were no other choice but to improve and to realize the success of all goals? Once accepted, this concept allows changes to become instantaneous.

Suggestion –
Complete Destiny

You've always known the old days and the unpleasant ways would soon be over, and whether it's right now, with some aspects let go of into the past, better and instead, now you now embrace your complete destiny of higher wisdom, better behavior, and the release of the old ways, feeling so completely relieved, supported, doing properly, living differently, behaving, healthier, as a greater sense of inspirational empowerment and inner and outer peace now your own, free of . . . (any and all desire to smoke anything whatsoever; old ways of eating that no longer support you and are boring and even silly; giving your power away to stressful situations and circumstances, now more empowered within yourself to rise above, etc.)

Insight –
Laughing at What Was Once the Monster

If the challenges in the past become laughable, any challenges can become more easily risen above and superseded.

Suggestion –
Laughing at What was Once the Monster

The greater the challenge, the more calm, relaxed and focused you become; knowing, active empowerment guided by mighty inner wisdom, life force and strength make your past and its most challenging moments so easily released and forgiven, so powerfully risen above, challenges now resolved and resolving, practically laughable.

Insight –
Subconscious Refocusing on Assets Rather than Deficits

All too often through conditioning brought on by life experiences, assumptions are accepted usually in a negative mode. Over time this becomes a subconsciously instilled habit. When empowering the client, it is critical to suggest reorientation of these tendencies toward something positive and beneficial to promote improvements. Knowing and appreciating their best aspects and assets, a change within internal communication can take place, arising greater self-esteem and self-confidence, more easily generating drive and determination toward self-improvement.

Suggestion –
Assets Rather than Deficits

Whatever any challenge in the past was, you now recognize and appreciate the true fact you have always survived, but even better right now within this ever-improving chapter of your life, you are fully choosing to thrive, choosing to live, you are doing everything and anything it honestly takes to break through and thrive step-by-step to ultimate success, activating inner power and your very best assets, achieving your goals unbeatably.

Insight –
Love as an Unstoppable Force of Life Transformation

It is been said that God is love. It has been said there is no greater force in the universe than love. In time, love heals all things. It has been said love heals all. It has been said love heals all wounds. Love can transform anything.

By definition, there is a wide variety of different things people call love, and a wide variety of people see love in a wide variety of ways—everything from love of God, love of self, love of life, love of family, the love of a parent, love of a spouse, romantic love, love of a child, love of friends, as well as love for animals, places, events, food, work, leisure activity, talent, hobbies moments of love remembered, and so many things to love. The list can go on and on.

Utilizing the concept of self-loving, self-appreciation, and loving one's self better than ever, allowing backsliding to take place as perhaps within the past, while building greater self-love and self-respect as the foundation for transformation, uses love as a source of transformation.

Suggestion –
Love as an Unstoppable Force

In this new and better chapter of your life, you remain loving yourself better, in all things great and small, you are doing better, feeling better while rising above any and all challenges more easily. For in this place, you are loving yourself enough and even better and beyond, while generating the flexibility of wisdom and compassion to yourself, to stay free and liberated, forever through your self-love to where you need to be and to forever live in this brand-new and forever better beneficial masterpiece chapter of your life, always moving forward, breaking through unbeatably.

Suggestion –
Love as an Unstoppable Force -Parent – Child - 1

As you would do almost anything to better love and protect your children, so too does your automatic mind now focus, and actively work out and appreciate loving yourself enough to improve, release the past, and better love and protect yourself, following through to break through ultimate success, more motivated and empowered, breaking through into achievement of any and all goals, both great and small, while activating limitless success in any and all things you seek to achieve most especially. . .

Suggestion –
Love as an Unstoppable Force -Parent – Child - 2

For the love of myself, for the love of my son, my days of smoking, forever done.

Suggestion –
Love as an Unstoppable Force -Parent – Child - 3

For the love of myself, for the love of my daughter, finished with smoking, I'm better now drinking water.

Insight –
Better Self-Appreciation and Self-Respect - 1

Suggesting better self-appreciation and self-respect, appreciating and respecting oneself enough to step forward to create improvements as necessary and to remain free of ever backsliding again, by treasuring, appreciating and respecting oneself to generate better options and choices, better habits, impulses and movement, better steps forward, better results are more easily achieved.

Suggestion –
Better Self-Appreciation and Self-Respect - 2

As you now have come into your own power, achieving knowingly your own success, you instill a better sense of self-appreciation coupled with self-respect enough to now know better, choosing better, behaving better, succeeding better, achieving and thriving as you have unbeatably stepped out to knowingly do, as you step forward to generate improvement moving only forward, as better steps forward yield better results more easily yet permanently achieved.

Insight –
Excuse Management –Kicking Excuses to the Curb - Once and for All

Many clients throughout their lives have learned to self-sabotage by getting creative, creating excuses, and developing subconscious strategies in order to set themselves up to fail. If your client is excuse-driven, perhaps giving them an excuse to succeed is undoubtedly a better way.

Suggestion –
Excuse Management

Kicking the old excuses out of your life, you recognize it's time to become true to yourself by becoming, forever remaining excuse-free, stepping up and completely motivated to meet obligations both great and small within your life, whether the house chores and responsibilities which need doing, practically anything, realizing little steps forward each day and night lead to more steps forward throughout the rest of your life. What a great reward. In fact, if excuses are ever made again, you will only make them in relation to putting aside the old ways in favor of these new more fulfilling and effective ones, actively bring your goals into your life, while completely releasing, relieving, forgiving, letting go of, and being done with, growing up and beyond, any and all old thoughts, feelings, ideas, memories or anything present or in the past, emotions, or anything in your life, either known or unknown to you, now being completely forgiven and released, grown up beyond, let go of, evaporated, dissolved, released, relieved yourself of any areas which have ever stood in your way, completely dissolving these right now blockages from the past, or even emotional sympathy. Completely within this new and energetically motivated yet unstoppable, brighter and better chapter, your completely well-deserved masterpiece chapter of your life and body, you are now forgiving, releasing, resolving, and even dissolving, moving forward from and away from, while cleverly relaxing through areas now finished, to find more joy in who you are as a human being, resolved to be living happier and thriving only at your very best.

Insight –
Creating a Dynamic Shift –
Shining Light where Darkness Once Was

Some of the behaviors from the past can be considered a form of shadow. Time to suggest a greater level of enlightenment, insight, understanding and wisdom are unstoppably taking place. Shining light into darkness alleviates the darkness, in fact shining light into any darkness generally clarifies and enlightens the situation.

Suggestion –
Shining Light

Living in the light of the better day, you remain living in the power of this better moment, sensing, even feeling the shift, as your automatic mind now easily vanquishes any and all shadows from the past, lighting up your present and future, creating a dynamic and beneficial shift to where it is you truly need to be, healthy, happy, safe, re-identified, doing and acting better, while always releasing, forgiving, gaining understanding and wisdom, yet choosing to learn better and achieve more, you adaptively and cleverly succeed in a place of higher understanding and higher light, re-identified better, your well-deserved enlightenment and freedom, now forever yours.

Insight –
Presenting the Subconscious with False Options

I have found many individuals, including those of a contrary nature or the doubtful ones seem to enjoy creating options. Those with a more negative orientation will assume failure and seek it out rather than expect better and break through. These people generate feelings of: "What's the use? I never win. I can never catch a break."

When dealing with such people, I give them options, which I've classified here. Options. Instead of giving them positive and negative, I give their subconscious mind a different perspective on options, as both are instead positive outcomes. In this way the subconscious mind is satisfied that there are options, but both options will only generate success and breakthroughs.

Suggestion - 1
False Options

As you relax deeper and further, floating, drifting, dreaming, deeper and further down, maybe even deeper than ever before, you now knowingly realize you only will either break through and succeed, or perhaps even better and instead, simply find yourself in some powerful moments of life transformation happy and free, while forever always remaining . . . (e.g.: smoke-free cigarette-free; lighter, thinner, healthier, better, more energetic, etc.)

Suggestion – 2
False Options

In this moment you will find you only break through and succeed, or perhaps simply and instead, step by step, become free of . . .(habit), living your dreams and generating only your very best.

Insight –
Internal Communication Change in the First Person

Guiding the subconscious mind to change one's own internal communication process in the first person is also another profound way of changing self-communication—motivating, while achieving ultimate goals. The way any of us think to ourselves is generally within the first person. Suggesting conversational change to something motivational and pivotal is a powerful pathway of change.

Suggestion –
Internal Communication Change

You may even find yourself thinking all of the following personal and profound now known inspired ideas as a fact, foundational life-truths – (I am so happy to have kicked cigarettes out of my life, what a relief! My health is better, I can breathe again, it's easy, I feel wonderful; eating better food makes me feel wonderful, and I am happy I made the all those necessary changes, I love feeling lighter and better . . .)

Insight –
Dissolving Disaster Thinking
Trusting in a Profoundly Better Tomorrow as a Usual Way of Life

A noticeable amount of clients have become accustomed to waiting for disaster to happen. Many of these clients seem to live their lives in a form of what could be called "red alert," constantly expecting the worst. They disaster-ize things that could turn out wonderfully, and through thinking this way, are more prone to stopping short of success in doing everything and anything it takes to succeed. Rarely do these people enjoy life, it seems their subconscious has been conditioned to expect bad things to happen, and as this is going on, they tend to magnetize shortfalls and disasters.

In reality, each of these people has risen above those disasters by virtue of the fact they have sought you out. Yet, from the subconscious their compulsive negative reconditioning continues. By suggesting away disaster thinking and generating trust in a profoundly better tomorrow is the usual way of life, repetitive negative and self-destructive patterns can dissolve.

Suggestion –
Trusting Profoundly

In this brand-new and better chapter of your life, you realize as the sun rises each morning and sets each night, so too has today taken care of you, just as every yesterday, tomorrow will do so as well. In this profound place of transformation and healing called your brand-new masterpiece life chapter takes complete care of you now more and more each and every day and night, as you right now come to recognize your life as a series of understandings, lessons, wisdom gained, while knowing from places deepest within your life, your world, even your universe, in this new place, evermore supportive, and as you relax barrier-free flowing forward, new and better more supportive thoughts, feelings, ideas, wisdom, understandings, even exceptional experiences guide your way into a more joyous and success-inspiring life.

Insight –
Action Orientation – Dissolving Procrastination

For clients who are somewhat convinced they've tried everything and nothing works for them, feeling in some way they are a special case, where others succeed, yet for them nothing works, procrastination and self-defeat create patterns of thinking that generate a defeatist way of life. Due to this predisposition, they create a way of thinking where motivation is lacking, excitement is practically nonexistent, procrastination is a habit and motivation is extremely necessary.

Over the years I have seen clients lose and damage reinforcement recordings, as well as develop a wide variety of excuses to generate failure. As their hypnotic coach, guide and motivator, it becomes necessary to build excitement, expectation, and moreover, get them to do their own reinforcement for their own benefit, often in spite of themselves. It is not enough that they booked a session, most people need motivation to keep going, even beyond the obvious benefit this success will bring them.

Suggestion –
Action Orientation – Dissolving Procrastination

Energetically stepping up to seize the moment in your life, you truly come to enjoyably unwinding, looking forward to reinforcing your hypnosis each and every night on your own, always with ever-increasing better results, truly looking forward to your relaxation time. You ever more completely enjoying the luxury of deep relaxation, as you ever increasingly and effortlessly generate well-deserved and wonderful success, slipping into hypnosis deeper, easier quicker and better, each and every time, generating better than wonderful results.

Insight –
Draining Away Disharmony and Imbalance

Thoughts both great and small can create feelings and a sense of energy in people, profound or subtle, positive or negative, life-affirming or life-denying. These thoughts and feelings are what have drawn your client into the position of acquiring habits and reactions, placing them in a position to clear up and beneficial habits, thoughts, feelings and reactions. Unless thoughts of disharmony and imbalance, negative feelings, unsupportive emotions, habits and a wide variety of relevant issues are forgiven and resolved, even drained off, they are likely to rise again. It is important to drain these off through suggestion. Then replace these negatives, these limitations with more positive and unlimited inspirations.

Suggestion –
Draining Away Disharmony and Imbalance

It's almost like someone from deep, deep inside of you in this moment has opened a valve from deep, deep inside of you, draining away effectively any and all blockage and negativity energy, in fact, any and all shortfalls, disharmony and imbalances are now easily drained away. Clearing now, what fills up the space right now, is a beneficial and well-deserved, beautiful energy, an energy of inspired and creative life-force, strength, skillful adaptability, unconditional love, and inner light, which easily refills, in endless supply, focusing you, rejuvenating you, and liberating your unbeatable mighty inner hero unstoppably.

Insight –
Release Generates Relief

It is also crucial for the client to have an improved sense of feeling, truly feeling these changes are real and are in fact taking place. Bringing transition, transformation and beneficial change to a level of feeling brings comfort, and a sense that regular improvement is continuing perpetually.

Suggestion –
Release Generates Relief

Your mind now easily and powerfully generates any and all powerfully effective sensation or feeling, pace or plan you now or will ever need to create adaptive and breakthrough success, putting down past burdens, lighter and feeling free, releasing and relieved, in ways both known or unknown to you, ahh, what a relief.

Insight –
Purposely Driving Forward Success

I have found it productive to continually push forward their success, in spite of events and circumstances, even beyond back-sliding and the occasional doubt. Your client's inner hero has, in this brand-new chapter of their life, no room for doubt, except to see how useless doubt is and how easily risen above, they now are driven while moving onward into their own success.

Suggestion –
Purposely Driving Forward Success

For the mightier the challenge you ever once had, in a previous chapter of your life, you truly come to know it's both now and forever done, released, and forgiven. However it once was, in this new chapter of your life, the more formidable and mighty you are and the more empty and nothing that former challenge now is, as you self-assuredly stand there proudly and laugh at how easy the past is released and how much better things have become. So much more effective you are and you remain.

Insight –
Knowing and Living from a Higher Truth

In a mindset of more actively effective functional wisdom and understanding, people tend to know better and do better. However, keeping their focus on these understandings and achieving such goals, looking forward, remembering and repeating a better truth, while often shedding the past and negative memories and experiences, replacing them with better ideas, greater truth, and living from the ideals of these greater truths and insights.

Most people I have met have not been trained to think this way, the world we live in conditions us to think in negative terms. Quite often it's easier to assume the worst about people, circumstances and events. This can be reinforced by news broadcasts, and society in general at times. Yet within your client's ability to transcend all of this, they now know better and live from a better place continually.

Suggestion –
Knowing and Living from a Higher Truth

All of you is now knowing, truly living from a higher truth, as anything you put your mind to, now more easily than ever before within your grasp, activated into the world around you. Heroically freed, you now venture ever onward to seize your success and make it one with you, feeling and knowing, actively making success yours, while enjoying feelings of satisfaction and success, as a deep and true part of you now knows this and makes this all your very own. Having done all of the necessary work, succeeding brilliantly. The truth real, this is yours, certain and sure.

Insight –
Succeeding as if Life Depended on these Changes

If your client were driven to succeed as if their life depended upon it, would a successful outcome motivate them to drive and succeed as never before? More than likely. In a great many cases of people I have worked with over the years, especially many of those who have come in for session work with illnesses connected to their habit, from smokers medically ordered to quit smoking, to morbidly obese individuals being medically required to lose weight before surgery, and other similar circumstances, in these cases it's more obvious to some greater extent their lives depend on the success of these sessions.

Yet even in regular weight loss sessions and smoking cessation, even stress management or even helping someone achieve a better night of sleep, quite often in some way the benefit our work brings to their lives is incalculable. To get a single parent or grandparent rid of cigarettes, helping extend their lives to be there the day of their child's wedding, as I see it, is something no price paid for a session really covers. When a habit has stopped and is forever transitioned away from, something transformative and truly amazing is taking place.

When I host a session I work as if each client's life depends on that very session. In every session, I let the client know I want results of them even more than they do, and am working hard to achieve this objective as a commitment to my client and my goal.

Suggestion –
Succeeding as if Life Depended on these Changes

You quit smoking right now as if your life depended on it. Free and clear, happy and content, you've never felt so good!

Insight –
Simply Finished and Done

In most everyone's life there's been a moment of putting your foot down, and simply moving on. A time when someone was just simply finished, left and went forward. That time is now.

Suggestion –
Simply Finished and Done

As when so many times in the past when you put your foot down, or instead when something was simply finished, over and done, right now, simply just moving on, you absolutely are and remain finished forever with (name habit), successful, motivated and free.

Insight –
Life Reset to Truly Release the Past

If people only came with a series of circuits and switches from deep inside of them, the goals our clients seek to achieve would be instantly more easily attainable and achievable. Yet, as hypnotists, are we not capable of suggesting this as if actual?

Suggestion –
Life Reset to Truly Release the Past

You may even come to realize your life has been completely reset in your favor. In this place of deep rest, relaxation and unstoppable inspiration, you know it's almost as if someone has actively reset a switch, a dial, thermostat, or computer of some kind, easily allowing you to release the past and any and all of its blockages now dissolving and dissolved completely, while generating more optimal outcomes for your future and most especially your point of power which is right now, freed forever of (name habit).

Suggestion –
Life Reset

It is as if someone has reset a ultimately powerful switch, a dial, a thermostat, or a computer from deepest within you, resetting you, retuning you, recalibrating you, to a better place, your very best success now rising to the top unbeatably.

Insight –
Covert Confusion Suggestions

I'm a fan of using covert hypnosis suggestions, which can include a wide variety of techniques to slip under your clients' radar, to inspire and generate breakthrough success, especially in spite of resistance, known or even unknown to your client.

The goal here is to get subconscious mind working in harmony with the suggestions. Often this can take shape by using an incorrect word, or changing the order of the words in a sentence, which then forces the subconscious to reformat and reformulate the sentence into something actively viable.

Suggestion –
Covert Confusion

You know, you don't know, what it was you think you knew, so now better instead, you now know what it is to know, well now knowing all of this, you now just know.

Suggestion –
Covert Confusion - 2

Knowing this now for you, you now know this to be true.

Insight –
Shutting Down the Mill – Turning Off Struggle

Another predilection generating blockage is mulling over changes, feeling overwhelmed, throwing hands in the air and saying, "It's too much struggle, I am forever trapped." These ideas can run over and over again, mulling around in their heads, most often subconsciously. We are in a unique position to stop this while getting clients to treat themselves better.

Suggestion –
Turning Off Struggle

The days of mulling over ideas of limitation and struggling over, finished, past, done, outgrown, now powerfully, pleasantly forgiven and completely released into the past chapter of your life, forever done. Should you ever think about them again, you will smile to yourself warmly, feeling a warm heart, and more content and better knowing mind, in glowing knowing wisdom, as you now recognize you have outgrown and risen above these things, so much better you are and you remain, having forever moved on.

Insight –
Truisms to Achieve a New and Better Supporting Truth

Your clients' new way of living is actually a now known truth and reality. As this new improving reality is now accepted by the subconscious mind, changes and improvements are more powerfully and smoothly taking place, oftentimes consciously unknown to your client.

A new day of better and more empowering truth via suggestion drives forward success inspirationally. In this method mixing other facts known to be true, say several truths mixed together, and at the end of those thoughts, coupling with a new and better truth, generates more complete transformational change.

Suggestion –
Truism

Just as the sun comes up in the morning shining a higher light, and just as the sun sets in the evening, and just as the stars shine bright at night, and as this world moves around the sun, so too do you eternally enrich and improve. Now knowing this to be true for you, you break through, free of old habits, and release (old habits). Truly now within your ever improving and inspirationally supportive life, your world, your universe, inside and out remain shining bright, as you are more easily feeling serene, as you now know profound improvements taking place. In knowing, glowing wisdom of success, so inspired, you now live.

Insight –
Strategies For Success Automatically Formulate

It also works wonders when you suggest to the subconscious automatic strategies for success are automatically formulating. Harnessing the power of the subconscious mind to work in your clients' favor generally creates amazing improvements even beyond anything anyone could ever consciously cook up.

Suggestion –
Strategies For Success Automatically Formulate

Whether you realize it or not, your automatic and dynamic mind, inspired, now forever working in your favor, while automatically generating and creating completely effective, well-placed, carefully constructed amazing improvements, which although first not immediately noticed, are in effect and making you feel wonderful, each of these success effects may even surprise you.

Insight –
Their Days of Simply Surviving Over, the Days of Living Now Theirs.

Establishing fluid success is essential to habit improvement. Struggle as a concept needs to become a thing of the past, overcome, released, forgiven, moved beyond and above. Suggestion alone without reward restrains success, keeping clients unmotivated and limited. Suggestion coupled with reward can be essential to beneficial success.

Suggestion –
Days of Living

In this new and better place, you are somehow always getting to, yet have truly arrived, beyond survival, forever better learning to absolutely live and thrive, goal realization achieves better living, better life.

Insight –
Creating an Effectively Supportive Emotional Base

It is useful and worthwhile to ask the subconscious mind to generate supportive emotions, feelings, thoughts, drive, success-driving insights and inspiration to make this new chapter of living better-feeling and more worthwhile.

Suggestion –
Creating an Effectively Supportive Emotional Base

All that you do, more actively supportive and upbeat, even happy emotional feelings, thoughts, and inspirations, unconditionally support profound improvement, now driving you forward while guiding your way into the very best chapter of your life, and you feel ever–better, even wonderful, (name new habit/behavior).

Insight –
Serenity and Relaxation as Reinforcement

While helping to generate a brand-new and better chapter of someone's life, free of old habits, suggest they see this place of harmony and serenity as a new place to live. Within this place, they move beyond survival patterns and thinking, not only just living here but rather thriving, truly living, enjoying life more, while forever refining improvements.

Suggestion –
Serenity and Relaxation as Reinforcement

You will find within your mind, your world and your very life, within this brand-new and forever place, your life, a more restful, serene and stress-free you thriving, a place within you almost contemplative. Your automatic mind so relaxed, yet keyed and attuned, more restful and more rested, automatically more easily enabled to skillfully work out things to your thriving maximum benefit with ease, even masterfully, keeping you free of old ways while keeping you safe, calm, focused, liberated from the past, better inside and out, firmly and keenly, serenely forever into your new and better.

Insight –
Laughter as a Reinforcement Trigger

I've also successfully used laughter as an instant reinforcement trigger. Statistics vary, but I have read the average child laughs perhaps hundreds of times during the course of the day, while the average adult only laughs about six times per day. Laughter has been shown to release a wide variety of beneficial chemicals produced by the body, including endorphins, has been shown to stimulate the immune system, slow aging, lift spirits, release stress, increase intelligence, along with a wide variety of additional benefits, some possibly yet to be discovered.

As a part of the package of beneficial improvement I am seeking to activate within the client, I will also suggest a more upbeat attitude, laughing off the smaller challenges when appropriate, and each and every time laughter occurs, all suggestions, adaptations and other benefits are instantly reinforced. I generally tie this with seeing a particular color or object. Often the color of choice is red, as red is a color most of us are forced to look at, from car tail-lights, to stop signs, to traffic lights and the list goes on and on. Objects include wristwatches, shoes, pens, business cards or even things like cigarettes or food someone is seeking to move away from as part of a weight-loss program.

Two or three colors also work. Beyond a few simple choices, adding additional colors and textures becomes counterproductive.

Occasionally a client will suggest another color based on the color of the room, colors on a computer screen, particular types of metal such as kitchen appliances, to name just a few. I suggest when they see this particular color or object, and *only when appropriate*, they will to begin to smile, giggle, even laugh, and as they do, suggestions are further reinforced.

Suggestion –
Laughter as a Reinforcement Trigger

You will come to know the color X (object X)- this is going to become more obvious, more dynamic and inspiring to you than you can even imagine, almost like it's jumping out at you, right into your face, right into your eyes, always making you smile, sometimes even giggle and even laugh really, really hard, just like a little kid. It is going to seem more soothing, inspiring, reinforcing, just more relaxing and more unstoppably inspiring to you, almost as if it's jumping out at you, right into your face, right into your eyes, and only when appropriate, funnier and funnier. Each & every time you see the color X, you are going to be more inspired and unstoppably determined to effectively and adaptively achieve your goal of [becoming remaining smoke-free cigarette-free – lighter and thinner, healthier and better, etc.]. As you notice this remarkable color X (or object) it profoundly inspires you to be more successful in all that you want to accomplish, wish to accomplish, can, will and in fact do unstoppably and effectively accomplish, more relaxed, inspired, creatively determined and unstoppably successful than ever before.

Insight –
Objective Situational Reinforcement via Laughter

Just as the hypnosis stage show suggestions can make any object funny via suggestion, in clinical hypnosis both the object and the laughter can be used as reinforcement triggers, to both effectively and adaptively reinforce session success.

Suggestion -
Objective Situational Reinforcement via Laughter

Each and every time you see a wristwatch [cell phone clock], it seems to jump into your face, into your eyes, pleasantly surprising you, perhaps making you smile, giggle, or maybe even laugh, laugh out loud, just like a little kid, eight years old, laughing at the funniest movie you ever saw, getting funnier and funnier.

Each and every time you look at your own wristwatch [cell phone clock], you are truly more calm, and serene, more happy abundantly all over, more relaxed, and more assured of the very best chapter of your life beginning, one in which you are and you effectively remain, (smoke-free, cigarette-free – or – lighter, thinner, healthier, better, with a much higher metabolism, etc.).

[When the client laughs after being brought out of hypnosis at your wristwatch, they know something has taken place, something is different, and just maybe, important and forever life-changing improvements have taken place].

Insight –
Consistent Subconscious Adaptation for Reinforcement

Get the subconscious mind adaptively working on blockage relief, release, removal and resolution on multiple levels, physically, emotionally, mentally, and in every way a human being thinks, can act or even react, while adapting, all while suggestions initially given, moment to moment, adaptive and continually self–refined. As the subconscious is active within a person, it is beneficial to keep it working on successful breakthrough progress, orienting and reorienting adaptation on a consistent basis for fluid self–reinforcement.

Suggestion –
Consistent Subconscious Adaptation for Reinforcement

As only your very best is rising to the top, for you now unbeatably, in this brand-new and better self-fulfilling empowerment moment of your life, in ways known but moreover generally unknown to you, your automatic and dynamically powerful subconscious mind is consistently refining and adapting any and all aspects necessary to keep you happy, safe, while ever more completely achieving your goals successfully, while calm and peaceful, even serene, while ultimately knowing you are achieving, always automatically working out everything and anything to achieve maximum benefit and success in ways now unbeatable. This now you know forever, knowing profoundly.

Insight –
Reinforcing Inspired Greatness

Suggesting your client's subconscious mind reinforce on an unknown yet active basis within the very best of your client's abilities, aspirations, insights, reactive adaptations, sensing and undeniable knowledge of improvement, and within the same scope of energy, drive, and unstoppable determination, as if from others who have succeeded in releasing a blockage or an old habit, as they are doing, as if that other person's success is now theirs, can work as reinforcement to achieve inspire greatness on a self-perpetuating basis.

Suggestion –
Reinforcing Inspired Greatness

As if all the inspirational energy of your greatest aspects, or other people you've observed, is now unstoppably yours, right now, rising up unbeatably to solve, resolve, releasing the past unpleasantness, as you move forward only as your goal achievement is at hand. As you now make any and all of this your very own, you are fully knowing this, absolutely, in both heart and mind. Most especially whenever challenged in any way, only your very best rises energetically and unbeatably to the top, instantly reinforcing your very best functioning success strategies, improving all you seek, as new ways, better habits, ever-improving ideas, and inspirational greatness, for you now are knowing better, you now fully live better, while in this new place, more free, thriving and inspired, absolutely actively enabled to achieve your goal, any goal, for this place where you now and forever live, more free, always better achieving.

Insight –
To Permanently Prevent Backsliding
Inspiration and Driven Determination to Automatically Overwhelm All Past Issues

One of the most prevalent client fears is backsliding stumbling, slowing, or even halting forward progress in habit release. How often have clinical hypnotists heard, "What if it doesn't work?" It is essential to continue the client's forward progress in ways unbeatable, automatically effective, while rising up to adaptively meet all challenges, moving forward in the true knowledge goal achievement is at hand, while old habits release. They now live in a brand-new and better place, living a greater truth, utilize necessary knowledge and wisdom, easily overcoming backsliding. When suggestions are crafted properly, even formerly stubborn challenges seem silly or a non-thought.

Suggestion –
Automatically Overwhelm All Past Issues

As you now have come to notice, recognize, realize or somehow instead truly understand all of this as a new foundation, or moreover even better know, as an unstoppable new sense within you has awoken, a boundless energy of a more felt and complete inspiration, a sense of driven forward determination, effectively active, which supports you and all you seek to achieve. As you are now more completely enabled to rise up to automatically overwhelm any and all past challenges or frictional moments as truly courageous and inspired, even driven. Any and all of past challenges now seem to be dissolving and melting as feelings even memory, so very resolved, so very solved, so risen above, so overwhelmed, as you now, the mighty one, so forever empowered and inspired. Your forward movement toward your goal and your freedom, every step towards a better way of life and living, the choice you lovingly give yourself, living from and now and forever know.

Insight –
Expectation - Being the Miracle

Most clients are seeking to achieve what some might call a miracle. Let's face it, for someone who's tried perhaps dozens of times to quit smoking, or to shed excess weight, or overcome with what seems to have become an unshakable habit, or any other the wide variety of sessions we host, although hoping for a change, the realization of such profound change for some clients seems more of a dream, perhaps a magic trick or even a miracle.

Sometimes, we even work with people who ask us to help them succeed even in spite of themselves. Yet so very often, we do succeed in providing amazing breakthrough help. So suggest the subconscious mind look forward to and expect nothing less than the profound change, even what might be called a miracle, while seeking out such benefit, your suggestions create it.

Suggestion –
Expectation - Being the Miracle

As so very many who come for hypnosis generally break through and succeed, the profound improvement and change you look forward to, simply now even as you exhale, has somehow become your own. With each and every breath you take and with each and every beat of your heart, is as if the breath is further ushering you in to a life full of profound change and the successful realization you once sought, even the miracle change, is now your own. Your creative mind, with every thought, breath, and heartbeat, truly makes this ever more so, as you now know.

Insight –
Self-Sabotage?
In Spite of and Because of

For any client practicing forms of self-sabotage, it is crucial to move your client past this limitation mindset. A technique that works effectively is reversing back upon itself the techniques they been using to hurt themselves, keeping themselves stuck in a habit. In spite of this game, or because of it, as a hypnotist, we have the complete leverage to turn this around.

Suggestion –
In Spite of and Because of

You succeed here, in powerful ways, which seem to be slipping through into the reality around you, in spite of, and even because of, times in the past you once blocked yourself. In this place, more powerful your resistance once was, the more you succeed. The more you succeed, the more dissolved your resistance becomes.

Insight –
Contrarians?
This in Fact is True – Not Because I Say So

Some clients are counter hyper–reactive to positive suggestions simply because they are of a contrary mindset or simply are used to rebelling against authority. No one is going to tell them what to do, not even themselves.

Suggestion –
This in Fact is True – Not Because I Say So

Any and all of the beneficial changes are in fact true, as you now know them to be, *not because I say so,* but rather instead and because they just seem to be happening to your well-deserved benefit on your own, in spite of or because of any resistance past, present, or future. Out of your own way once and for all you are and you remain, achieving beneficial success.

Insight –
Blocked?
Blockage Dissolving and Release

The various blockages, both known and especially unknown, which the client has set up to keep themselves trapped, work stronger than any superglue. So carefully complex, elusive and constructed as so many of these blockages tend to be, so request the subconscious mind's assistance in blockage alleviation. Without blockage alleviation, client improvement is tenuous, difficult, and has a high probability for backsliding, sliding back into the past.

Suggestion –
Blockage Dissolving and Release

You have already, creatively and effectively, in ways automatic and meaningful, you relax deeply within, into yourself, and into your life, effectively and adaptively, while forgiving, releasing, evaporating and dissolving any and all old habits, actions, reactions, thoughts, feelings, or imprints, while powerfully reconfiguring, adopting and adapting new and better health supporting habits and ways of living, thriving, and succeeding, shinier and new in heart and mind, effectively rising above any and all past challenges.

Insight –
Blockages Become Support

Another highly useful method in blockage alleviation is reversing blockages back upon themselves to collapse those blockages.

Suggestion –
Blockages Become Support

Things once a hindrance, now become a means of support, turned around back from the past, upon themselves, as they collapse, long-lasting freedom, you are better supported, completely freer, living well.

Insight –
Establishing a New Foundation - Self-Motivation

Reconstructing foundations clears and opens a place to rebuild, a place to restart, establishing a new foundational base. This is important to set up subconsciously when reformatting your clients' habits onto the path of beneficial improvement. Active self-assurance as a form of self-motivational coaching subconsciously establishes the client's subconscious mind as self-motivating. Continual self-motivation is also a potential key to success, especially when circumstances arise challenging habit improvements.

Suggestion –
Establishing a New Foundation - Self-Motivation

Self-assured and self-reassuring, beyond even what these words mean to a more meaningful and powerful place of pivotal improvement and profound change, you actively and effectively remain. The imbalances are past now, reversed back upon themselves, collapsing them, in this masterpiece chapter resides truth as your strength, affecting major habit improvements, in free-flowing adaptive wisdom as your profoundest truth. This wisdom giving your life and yourself new meaning to be at your very best.

Insight –
Forgiveness Motivation – Bringing Freedom

Should new moments of challenge to improvements arise, should old issues crop up, activating a sense of inspirational rewards to create freedom will continue motivating improvement and reinforcement.

Suggestion –
Forgiveness Motivation – Bringing Freedom

Absolute and complete forgiveness paves the road to a life better lived, health supporting habits filled with enjoyable freedom, so well deserved, alleviating imbalanced connections to the past, so you now know, you create this making easily yet effectively, just making it so.

Insight –
Loving Enrichment

The term enrichment is a bit of a subconsciously loaded term. Subconscious mind tends to hear the word *rich* rather than enrichment. Most of us would like to be richer than we are, whether it be richer monetarily, or better loved, blessed with true friends, better moments, or greater states of self-fulfillment. Another stream of consciousness to tap into for effective improvement.

Suggestion –
Loving Enrichment

Opening your heart to yourself more completely, self lovingly, your heart now more open to share your brightest, your best, and other aspects of the richness that is you, in the real and most truest sense of the word, your personal enrichment, now yours, experiencing greater joy.

Insight –
Benefit and Improvement Only

Suggestions need to be designed as adaptive and fluid to be more effective. As your client post-session reinforces their improvement process via self-hypnosis, improvements generate complete benefit, and will continue each time the process is performed, adaptations taking place as changes might be needed. It's important to suggest the process as an enjoyable one, something to look forward towards keeping reinforcement motivation high.

Suggestion –
Benefit and Improvement Only

You will only receive powerful and precise, highly effective, beneficial improvements in the most correct, potent, extremely effective, powerfully correct and fluidly adaptive ways from this. You are easily going into this wonderful relaxation state faster, deeper, stronger and better, with more limitless results, greater impact, in more unlimited dynamic ways every time you repeat this extremely enjoyable, wonderfully effective dynamic, highly effective and precise exercise.

Insight –
Environmental Factors as Reinforcement Triggers
Perpetual Environmental Sound Reinforcement

Your client's hearing is always on. In most anyone's environment there are sounds from outside or inside their home, workplace, car, or anywhere else they exist. These sounds can also be heard while sleeping, one proof of this is an alarm clock waking someone up. Why not use environmental sounds as reinforcement modalities?

Suggestion –
Perpetual Environmental Sound Reinforcement

The whole world works to support you in all of this, every sound, every noise that you hear from outside, including sirens, car horns and car alarms, (barking dogs, etc.) each and every time you hear them, they instantly reinforce any and all of your very best benefits. Even telephone noises, every time you hear them are instantly reinforcing all of this, most especially your freedom and liberation from . . . *(e.g. smoking, overeating, holding weight - gaining weight, your old habit, your fear, etc.)*

Insight –
Activating Unstoppable Improvement

There are a great many twists and turns your client can experience in their day-to-day lives that can challenge improvements, generating backsliding into old habits and impeding progress toward any given goal. Suggesting their subconscious mind generate an unstoppable force of life improvement, always functioning in their favor now, as a resource of adaptive reinforcement, a greater sense of being true to one's goals, can easily assist in more fully reaching goal achievement.

Suggestion –
Activating Unstoppable Improvement

In fact you feel like you've got the whole world in the palm of your hand. You are a breakthrough winner. An unstoppable force of unstoppable life improvement from deep within you has been forever activated. Your awareness grows, your life expands, you are both now and forever free and you truly know it.

Insight –
Conflict Resolution

Conflict, either external or internal, can easily arise as an impediment to breakthrough success. External excuses based on conflict can be connected to numerous factors, from relationships, to work or school environments, home, life, and the list goes on. Internal conflicts can arise from your client meeting to more fully embrace changes and improvements, to patterns, thoughts, memories long buried and consciously forgotten. Sometimes internal conflicts are rooted in the client knowing where they are today, unsure of what an improved life will feel like tomorrow, especially if challenges arise. The idea of *being comfortable in their own misery* comes to mind. When setting the mind to automatic self-improvement, suggest adaptive detachment from such conflicts, so clearing the road toward improvement then becomes essential.

Suggestion –
Conflict Resolution

And your self-confidence, self-esteem and inner strength immediately increases. As you relax, you more effectively detach completely from all conflicts, frictions and disharmonies, relief, feeling forever free. You are empowered, successful and liberated. With every breath which you take, with each and every beat of your heart, your strength and dynamic empowerment increases, making you more effective, as more profoundly every suggestion, especially all adaptations your mind resolves, generating goal success, instant activation, amazing and impressing everyone, especially even you!

Insight –
New Empowerment

Instilling a sense of personal empowerment, the ability to take on and rise above almost anything, adaptively, the energetic ability to achieve, driven, motivated, and ever-improving, while more effectively achieving goals and activating greater success builds inspiration.

Suggestion –
New Empowerment

You begin to take even better care of yourself, re-identifying and re-defining yourself as achieving a new happier, energetic and lighter-hearted person, allowing newer and more empowered thoughts and inspired feelings of success, healing, wellness, breakthrough and health, fluid effective adaptability, clear focus, to each and every day profoundly expands, building within you like a giant reservoir of limitless energy, allowing you and all of your very best to rise up, bringing out a more well-deserved, greater and truer reality, in which you live, better life habits begin, where you are and forever remain effective, whole, calm, comfortable, successful, lighter, better, more complete.

Insight –
Your Client's Subconscious as an Unstoppable Force

Suggesting their subconscious become an unstoppable force of improvement can generate more unstoppable improvements, adaptively and automatically. Beyond the unstoppable force, the subconscious can be suggested to be their own internal coach, while eliminating and alleviating excuses and blockages, and instead generating beneficial action.

Suggestion –
Unstoppable Force

Your desire to succeed becomes a passion, your passionate desire becomes a truly committed unstoppable force, as more and more completely, both each and every day and night, you overwhelmingly succeed in truly inspired, effective, creative, amazing and successful ways. Forever super motivated, while effective, flowing forward into a better you, while relaxing into this remarkable brand-new better chapter of your life, winning in the most profound ways! You have no idea how easy this is going to be for you.

Insight –
Use of the Word No

By using the word *no* in the suggestion above, the subconscious tends to eliminate the word *no*, translating instead into – You have an idea how easy this is going to be for you.

Suggestion – 1
Use of the Word No

You have no idea how easy this is going to be for you.

Suggestion 2–
Use of the Word No

You may as yet have no idea how smooth your transitions into better habits and a better, healthier life are going to be.

Insight –
True Reconditioning and Redefinition

By suggesting a client expansion reconditioning toward more unlimited success, and a redefinition beyond old and no longer useful limits, to live a more essentially healthier life, which evolves evermore, improving issues and challenge resolution, clears impediments both known and unknown, as motivation drives your client forward into ever-increasing success.

Suggestion –
True Reconditioning and Redefinition

With each and every breath you take, you are powerfully liberating the inspired feelings, energy and sensations associated with these following thoughts, ideas and concepts into a vitality, ever-improving, precisely in your favor, effectively motivated and ever-evolving, more profoundly true reconditioning and more expanded redefinition of who you are, living better, better habits. In this place, where you live from, how you respond and whom you grow forever to being in your life. All of this getting you forever unbeatably to wherever it is you best need to be, freedom now yours as you are feeling wonderful and forever improving by becoming *(name the desired goals, attributable feelings, actions and reactions you wish to instill).*

Insight –
Achieving Subconscious Agreement

Suggest the subconscious mind agree to step out of the way of blocking behavior, motivated by memories, feelings, ineffective thought patterns, to instead become in complete agreement with all beneficial improvements being made, effectively reinforcing adaptive and effective lifelong success.

Suggestion – 1
Achieving Subconscious Agreement

(While they are deeply hypnotized) Nod your head for me because you now and forever truly know that you've forever relaxed your way into a brand-new and better chapter of your life and really know that all of this is true. In this place you are

truly working in your favor, yes this is true. *(Wait for their nod and continue).*

Suggestion – 2
Achieving Subconscious Agreement

(While they are deeply hypnotized) Nod your head for me because you know that this is true. *(Wait for their nod and continue).*

Insight –
Head Shaking and Nodding As Posthypnotic Reinforcement Triggers

Utilizing body motion as a reinforcement trigger will tend to reinforce session suggestion success in self-perpetuation as your client lives their life. During anyone's daily conversations, shaking when they know or nodding one's head yes can be done dozens or hundreds of times a day as a form of nonverbal communication, often as a subconscious reaction. Why not use this subconsciously driven automatic behavior as a posthypnotic instant reinforcement trigger? Harnessing this attribute as the source self-perpetuating reinforcement will generate amazing results in your client's life.

Suggestion – 1
Head Shaking and Nodding As Posthypnotic Reinforcement Triggers

For the rest of your life, whenever you shake your head no when appropriate, you, smiling inwardly to yourself, knowing you are saying no to all things in the past which ever lead you to become or remain (name habit). Each and every time you nod your head yes, you are saying yes to your brightest and best, and when appropriate smiling inwardly to yourself, knowing how much greater your life is, freer and better, having risen above any and all old ways into a healthier and better chapter of your life, (name, new ways of healthier habits; smoke-free, cigarette-free; lighter, healthier, thinner, better, higher metabolism; more calm and easier breathing, stress-free; able to relax and sleep better, enjoying better rest; etc.).

Suggestion – 2
Head Shaking and Nodding As Posthypnotic Reinforcement Triggers

Each and every time you shake your head no, you are saying no to your past and moving into a better day. Each and every time you nod your head yes, you are saying yes to a newer and brighter, happier and better X (smoke free, lighter, thinner, healthier and better you, etc.) chapter of your life. Now sure of yourself, you are unstoppable.

Insight –
Turning Resistance Around –Head Nodding

Using body movements such as head nodding can actively work to resolve resistance every time any resistance energy is present or building.

Suggestion –
Turning Resistance Around –Head Nodding

The more in the past you once resisted yourself, the more in the future you work unstoppably and effectively in your favor to cleverly, abundantly and forever succeed at this. Nod your head yes for me because you know it's true; each and every time you nod your head yes, you now more know this to be true.

Insight –
Improvement as Known Truth

As improvements are taking place, automatically, suggest a profound recognition of having reached a greater personal sense of truth, and self-support, in which any and all goals are more easily and forever achievable.

Suggestion –
Improvement as Known Truth

You trust in and truly know this fact: each and every moment rising up to be your best as your life is improving, as things get better and more surprisingly and astoundingly wonderful for you in each and every way.

Insight –
Self-Support

As your client post-session will be reinforcing their hypnosis and beneficial suggestions through their self-hypnotic process, the subconscious mind needs to remain ever self-supporting of these improvements.

Suggestion –
Self-Support

You are enjoyably relaxed while feeling a new, correct, truly profound sense of self-support from your life, urging you ever onward into a lifetime of clever, self-adaptive yet powerfully successful lifelong improvements.

Insight –
Action as Truth

When someone has fully resolved to make up their minds to move forward from something, they always will. They are now embracing a different truth.

Suggestion –
Action as Truth

Just as you've always done, you are taking effective action, now knowing new health-supporting habits to be true for you, while doing everything you've unstoppably put your mind to, to fluidly get the job done. In the most effectively efficient of ways, motivated to succeed brilliantly, just as you have always done, yet right now ever more effective, most especially

. . . (*quitting smoking forever, losing weight, reducing stress, etc.*).

Insight –
Full Life Improvement – Opening the Door

There can be so many aspects a client will never share with anyone, even from those they seek out for help. Generally the client isn't even consciously aware of these aspects. Suggesting the generation of inspired beneficial feelings will help drive forward achievements.

Suggestion –
Full Life Improvement– Opening the Door

As you become ever increasingly determined to feel good, you are surely feeling fine, unstoppably inspired, driven, wonderful, even fantastic. Ready for full life improvement, as if opening a door, you are now once and forever walking through, as you release your very best, powerfully achieving. So with each and every beat of your heart and with each and every breath that you take, you are relaxing deeper and further, as assuredly your whole life unstoppably forever improves.

Insight –
Emotional Imbalance Resolution

Whenever reacting to external and internal stressors, activating a calming breathing response can more effectively generate a sense of detachment and goal motivation, while keeping the client free of feeling overwhelmed. Doing so, your client remains more enabled to stick to improvements and achieve. Suggestions can overpower what once they found overwhelming, as breakthroughs are at hand.

Suggestion –
Emotional Imbalance Resolution

You will always remember to breathe deep and steady powerful soothing breath, an instantly calming, centering, stilling, harmonizing and balancing breath. By doing so, you are easily overcoming any and all challenges while releasing completely all fear, doubt, worry and panic. That which once overwhelmed you is now both easily and forever powerfully overwhelmed by you through the calming, restoring power of your breath, as you leave all imbalance and discomfort far, far behind you forever. All fear, doubt and panic are now and forever forgiven, easily risen above and overwhelmed by you, right now released, healed and vanquished.

Insight –
Reinforcement Improvement

Suggest the subconscious become an unstoppable force of self-reinforcing improvement, effectively keeping motivation levels high and energetic, most especially in the face of challenges.

Suggestion –
Reinforcement Improvement

Now that you are proud of yourself and evermore self-assured, you finding yourself evermore amazingly unstoppable at all of this. Feeling forever proud of yourself and permanently improving, taking your life back, enjoyably better habits, thoughts and feelings. Truly getting amazingly successful, reinforcement brings improvement, fluidly adaptive and precisely effective results now yours from this highly proficient and enjoyable experience, going back into this deeper, faster and even better results, every time you repeat this exercise, every time.

Insight –
Self-Support Whenever Challenged

Each of us has risen up to meet challenges, once we decided to create a mindset where things once considered problems are now reconsidered as a challenge. Once we had stopped giving away our power to a problem and decided to refocus our energies on overwhelming challenges, most generally succeed, and by doing so, often achieving some of our greatest moments.

Suggestion –
Self-Support Whenever Challenged

You are easily free of anyone throwing you off track by saying any words or even expressing any feelings, thoughts or actions which might stand in the way of habit improvement, your ultimate success. You are in fact feeling mighty, yet fluidly adaptive as you are easily rising above and masterfully transcending any and all old limits, while now forever thriving throughout this brand-new chapter of your life.

Insight –
Improved Outlook

Improving one's outlook toward the progress of success, and away from naysayers and blockage mentality frees the individual to generate modifications leading to breakthroughs. With this better outlook on the road ahead, achieving goals adaptively and wisely brings ease and permanence of transition.

Suggestion –
Improved Outlook

The truest and most real point of view which matters to you is your own. In the long run, the opinions of others are just that, just points of view, learned from, embraced, to be considered or rejected, or even to be just put aside. You put aside everything and anything which ever interferes with your ever-growing success. Whether it's opinions of others, stress, emotional feelings, mental patterns, even old blockages, even any challenges at all, most especially any and all of the moments which once caused you discomfort or distress, any feelings or thoughts of those moments turnaround favorably, generating a sense of comfort, peace, and trust. You as you now and forever know, you remain unstoppably becoming clearer, sharper, better, more fluid and adaptive, more flexible and unstoppably successful.

Insight –
Success via Self–Appreciation

A *can-do* sense and spirit is also highly motivational in breaking through and setting up the next chapter of an individual's life.

Suggestion –
Success via Self–Appreciation

Now you are learning to truly appreciate yourself, feeling capable. You can do anything you've now and forever set your unstoppable and effectively adaptive mind toward. Each and everything you do and on each and every breath and on each and every heartbeat, allowing clever adaptation, while succeeding at this as never before!

Insight –
Tranquility Reinforcement as Release

Generating a sense of inner peace and tranquility as a reinforcement tool is highly helpful. Resolving and releasing all or as many as possible negative habits, thoughts, feelings and ideas from the past frees up space for dramatic improvements. The sense of tranquility your client experiences when in hypnosis can be used to great benefit.

Suggestion –
Tranquility Reinforcement as Release

You have now made up your powerful, adaptive, highly effective mind, which is only now working in your favor, getting stronger, better and more effective at reducing and eliminating any and all disruptive thoughts, feelings, actions and reactions, which ever once caused you to *(name behavior)*, choosing now instead to deep breathe, to calm down and to thrive and succeed, forever fulfilling you. You are finding newer and better, more completely adaptive, fluid, skillful and eminently successful impulses and actions of reducing and even eliminating any and all old behaviors which ever once blocked you or stood in the way of your success, now in favor of the newer and better, well-deserved life and goal-supportive habits you now powerfully, effectively and adaptively create.

Insight –
Heartbeat and Breathing as Reinforcement

As long as anyone is alive, their heart must beat, and they must breathe. These autonomic processes are automatic, and when associated with self-improvement and benefit, can be used as ongoing permanent reinforcement. Since all of us have beating hearts and have to breathe, why not use heartbeat and breath in other ways, as reinforcement modalities?

Suggestion – 1
Heartbeat and Breathing as Reinforcement

With each and every beat of your heart and each and every breath you take, reinforcing inspiration, all of you and your powerful mind now easily reinforcing all of this in the most powerful and potently adaptive, yet highly effective of ways, day by day, night by night, moment by moment. You are glowing on the inside with all of the limitless energy of inspired success, making success your very own, on every heartbeat.

Suggestion – 2
Heartbeat and Breathing as Reinforcement

With each and every breath you take, and with each and every beat of your heart, you are powerfully liberating the feelings, energy, actions, habits, reactions, improvements and sensations associated with these following thoughts, ideas and concepts into a vital and profoundly true reconditioning and redefinition of who you are, where you live from, how you respond and whom you grow forever to be into your life: you are feeling wonderful and forever improving by becoming *(name the feelings, actions and reactions you wish to instill).*

Insight –
Clearing

Clearing out the old to make room for the new generates release and freedom from the past, paving the way for even more complete life improvement.

Suggestion –
Clearing

You now know it's time to clean up your life, so by relaxing further and deeper, so too are you resolving and dissolving all things which ever stood in your way, feeling unblocked and completely free. So too you are clearing as you are, right now and always, even forever, succeeding powerfully, adaptively, ever self-assured with ever-growing, more determined, creatively inspired, limitless and adaptively effective success.

Insight –
Beneficial Urge

Many people have urges, impulses, even reactions to situations in their lives which drive them to health and happiness damaging habits. Generating better urges and impulses via suggestion keeps them anchored within this masterpiece chapter of their lives, freed from the past and old habits they seek to resolve permanently.

Suggestion –
Beneficial Urge

In your past, one of your urges may have been *to (name behavior: smoke, overeat, etc.)*. However reset now to do better, both now and forever, your greatest urge, an unstoppable urge that's building up to being at least 178 times greater, growing ever stronger is to remain healthy safe and free *(name desired result: smoke free, cigarette-free, etc.)*.

Insight –
Craving Success

Old habits and urges can appear from cravings, which have been adopted over the years as a form of comfort for self-protection from factors both external and internal, leading to damaging habits. Replacing cravings through suggestion with a craving for success allows them to thrive at their very best.

Suggestion –
Craving Success

Your greatest and most overwhelming craving is to become and forever remain in better life habits, healthy, happy, free and safe. By extending your life in ways which work for you best, you cleverly remain self-supporting, craving and generating success, now and forever thriving within your very best.

Insight –
Re-association

Once unhealthy life habits have often been established, they can become associated with a stress break, comfort, or as a sense of reward. When breaking a habit, and ready to move on, a re–association with how destructive this habit or reaction actually was, instead reinstituting a better, improved response and reaction is a key for profound change.

Suggestion –
Re-association

The feel of a cigarette in your hand or mouth just feels so very uncomfortable, and now for you, it's just plain wrong! You've moved on and are now and forever free and happy, moving forever fluidly forward in your life.

Insight –
Release via Breath

Connecting subconscious release to breathing removes blockages and tears down barriers to success, liberating your client.

Suggestion –
Release via Breath

On each and every breath you take, automatically, most especially whenever challenged, and on each and every beat of your heart, you are releasing, relieved and released from past blockages which or might have ever once ever stood in your way. Blockage free, your future is bright and more unlimited now than ever before.

Insight –
Relaxing Through Barriers

Releasing old habits and patterns often requires giving up struggling when encountering an old barrier, now taking steps forward toward improvement in a smooth flowing manner, instilling a sense of relief.

Suggestion –
Relaxing Through Barriers

Completely relaxing into this, beyond your past, both now and forever more easily flowing forward and beyond any and all former barriers, you are both now and forever unstoppably succeeding, while flowing ever onward into your breakthrough success. Realizing and making your own right now a brighter and better life, new habits, evermore life-supporting. The past resolving, now resolved, you now relieved of the past to enjoy the present and your bright wonderful future.

Insight –
Utilizing Confidence to Dissolve Blockages

Being unsure and lacking confidence, most clients will stumble and fail to realize full potential, faltering far short of success. A confident client is a client more driven to success.

Suggestion –
Utilizing Confidence to Dissolve Blockages

You're smiling powerfully inside, in a warm profoundly knowing, glowing with most unstoppable confidence. You can actually imagine, even completely feel or simply just instead now truly know all old blockages and hindrances from your past are now just seemingly dissolving and melting away, success at hand now yours, as you have now moved into a new breakthrough chapter of your life. Feeling that unstoppable smile, nod your head yes. You really know you've succeeded here, out of your own way, rising up, you've succeeded! You are unstoppable, you are unbeatable, you are free, adaptive and self-supporting, you remain achieving, feeling fine!

Insight –
Confidence and Certainty

For many attempting to release a habit, it is easy to second-guess, especially after previous attempts at improvement has failed to succeed. This is especially reinforced after having attended to succeed through lesser effective methods in the past. Yet when someone is certain something is going to take place, those changes can more easily happen.

Suggestion –
Confidence and Certainty

You are now unstoppably smiling inside with a true and real knowing, in ever more, ever-growing, complete glowing confidence. You are sure of yourself and very certain of your improvements, more right now than any other time in your life.

Insight –
Inevitable Unstoppable Achievement

Suggest your client become an unstoppable force, getting the subconscious mind to accept the inevitability of breakthrough and success. As this concept is embraced as a powerful truth, anything, whatever it was, that stood in their way is dramatically less significant and more easily overwhelmed.

Suggestion –
Inevitable Unstoppable Achievement

As you now know a better truth, you are prevailing, dynamically and powerfully, ever more completely unstoppable in all that you seek to achieve. When you know the truth, you easily accomplish everything, unstoppable achievement is and remains inevitable, now yours.

Insight –
Dissolving Blockage

Completely dissolving blockages both known or unknown, generates release and relief, allowing only beneficial life improvements.

Suggestion –
Dissolving Blockage

Anything in your life, which ever once stood in your way, both known or unknown to you, has *Right Now*, just melted away and forever gone. You are now and forever free to unstoppably move on, excel and succeed at any and all motivations, actions needed to improve your life.

Insight –
Blockage Release Ease

Blockage release works easiest and best once struggle is reduced or eliminated as a blockage-driving factor. Energizing beneficial attributes to inspire and empower, fluidly adaptive, more easily generate change and improvement.

Suggestion –
Blockage Release Ease

You are effectively finding ways of removing, dissolving and releasing, more completely, in each and every way, the useless old past blockages, forgiving and releasing, most especially as you are relaxing deeper now and releasing everything and anything that ever stood in the way, as you relax, flowing ever onward, effective in ways both known or unknown, focused and fearless, dynamic and mighty, embracing success in sharing adaptability and improvement, activating change in your favor, driven and dynamic. As you are so mighty, powerful and effective at all of this, a sense of relief, complete resolution in this place of truth, in fact it's easy.

Insight –
Enjoyable Improvements

Inspirational improvements and smoother-running transitions, freeing your client of old habits, feelings and reactions can create greater effectiveness. Harmonizing these improvements makes the process more enjoyable, while generating a more motivated client, willing to more completely release struggle mentality while reinforcing, embracing improvements as enjoyable. Anything enjoyable is easier to do.

Suggestion –
Enjoyable Improvements

Truly you have enjoyed this beneficial, life-transforming relaxation. Your powerfully effective hypnosis session becomes only greater, evermore effective, as wonderful and valuable improvements now come into your life from this, even in surprising and spectacularly beneficial ways, evermore perfecting, powerfully improving all that you are, how you live and freeing up and powerfully activating only your very best effective inspirations and energies!

Insight –
Assuming New Truth

Something known as truth is easier to accomplish and remain with. Suggesting an assumed truth can represent a more complete and permanent, lifelong turnaround. As everyone knows . . .

Suggestion –
Assuming New Truth

As everyone knows, once you have unstoppably entered a brand-new, more viable and better chapter of your life, right here, things improve quickly and for only the very best. All habits, day-to-day functioning, and things in general improve easily. You are so sure of yourself, that's where you are now and happily remain forever, in ever growing and glowing confidence. You just now know, are breaking through, happening as if automatically, feeling wonderful. You know you are truly unstoppable in achieving your well-deserved success.

Insight –
Knowing

Knowing something is taking place removes all doubt from it, enabling profound improvements more substantially.

Suggestion –
Knowing

You might have once thought things might be impossible to improve or change, but you now, thinking better, you just know, *"I now know* I'm doing better and better and it's wonderful, easy and amazingly simple." *As always* my life is only getting better and better, I deserve this, it's now and forever mine as I make it happen, and so it is.

Insight –
Excuse Removal

For many, a habit that stands in the way of success is generating excuses. Many of these negatively based, limiting excuses prevent motion forward into this new beneficial chapter. But for so many, excuses become a way of life. Suggesting excuses instead now are to be made for success. Here, rather than generating shortfalls, misses, problems and failure, excuses are now turned around 180° to motivations and benefits.

Suggestion –
Excuse Removal

You succeed easily, now finding even better-motivated thoughts, feelings and ideas, even now finding powerful excuses to only succeed.

Insight –
Amazing Success and Ease

Transition toward beneficial improvements need not be difficult. Coupling improvements with a sense of astonishment, ease and success can allow heartfelt feelings of joy to arise and inspire.

Suggestion –
Amazing Success and Ease

It's really just amazing, astonishing, simple and how easy it is for you to just succeed with ease and . . . (melting off and keeping off, 71, 86 and even 99 lbs.; remaining forever, smoke free, cigarette-free, etc.).

Insight –
Victorious Realization

Coming to a greater victorious realization, greater truth and wisdom are embraced, unimportant old habits seem to fall away, as the concept of breakthrough becomes easier.

Suggestion –
Victorious Realization

You know, it's just amazing to realize right now, that you've relaxed your way into a newer and brighter better way, as a better attitude and victorious realization are achieved, as unimportant old habits just seem to fall away, breaking through is now easier [as the weight just seems to melt off as you easily melt away and release now, X Lbs.]

Insight –
Extreme Replacement

Turning the extremes they once went to into something beneficial, while supporting habit improvements.

Suggestion –
Extreme Replacement

You are forever free of past moments, of ever going to any kind of self-blocking extremes. Your new extreme is to extremely take the very best care of yourself and to simply thrive, working it all out surprisingly well, sticking now in your favor to what you know works and just doing it, impulsively drawn correctly forward to more limitless success, in amazing and even surprisingly easy ways.

Insight –
Forgiveness and Motivation

Hanging onto the past via critical past self-judgment impedes forward progress. In this new blank space in which can be built anything of better value, and enhanced, of a more unlimited and breakthrough nature, open for the client to have a release, building only their very best.

Suggestion –
Forgiveness and Motivation

You are now and forever in a more effectively motivated toward forgiving and releasing all of the unpleasant effects from your past (or some moment, childhood, any moment). You are now instead feeling upbeat even wonderfully reinvented, building only your very best, while having unstoppably entering a brand-new chapter of your life. In this place, always vigilant and remaining so super motivated, all of your very best actively supportive thoughts, feelings and self-correcting inspirations just rise to the top as the unwanted (habit or issue) just seems to melt off you. As you make the time to feel better about yourself and become heroically motivated to break though and succeed easily and amazingly at this, as eternal, forever and always.

Insight –
Success the Only Choice

The concept of success and failure are instilled in each of us from our earliest days, and reinforced within as we start school. Yet in our finest moments, as we had driven forward, doing our best at our best, we sometimes remember success is our only option.

Suggestion –
Success the Only Choice

In this brand-new and better chapter of your life, you only thrive and succeed at this. You break through easily and skillfully and even surprisingly, relieved and in true self-appreciation —as driven and effective, clever, fluid and adaptively working in your favor, knowing in this moment of truth success is your only option, right now, and you know these facts deeply and truly, forever, as your own.

Insight –
Self–Forgiveness for Release

Often each of us is our own harshest critic. Critical self-judgment keeps repeating and trapping clients in past situations and moments, keeping old habits—better released—instead, going strong. Self-forgiveness opens release.

Suggestion –
Self–Forgiveness for Release

You are forgiving and forgiven. Just letting go and forgiving any and all harshness, self-criticism going, now knowing you are evermore actively achieving, feeling whole, happier and better.

You are healing, you are healed, you are moving on into your very best in truly effective, supportive, better ways.

Insight –
Old Habits and Blockages Now Laughable – Reinforcement Trigger

It's difficult to give one's personal power away to something that's laughable. Tying in laughter and smiles as a reinforcement trigger, obviously unbelievably useful.

Suggestion –
Old Habits and Blockages Now Laughable– Reinforcement Trigger

In this brand-new and better chapter of your life, habits, ideas, feelings, memories, which ever once stressed you out as a challenge to improvement, even a blockage, so long ago, so much weaker, so much more resolved, becoming even laughable. It's almost as if a smile breaks out across your face, remembering those moments, because in these moments, you become, and you forever are, so much more now forever free, laughing at how easy it is to be.

Insight –
Emotional Self-Support

The emotional components of your client need to be self-supporting while generating improvements.

Suggestion –
Emotional Self-Support

Each and every thought, each and every feeling, in fact, each and every action or reaction you have or will ever have are now working unstoppably in your favor to break you through, better habits, better actions, reactions, truest freedom, and more completely improving your life.

Insight –
Now Finished

Whenever someone has simply gotten past something once and for all, they've moved on beneficially and completely, forever.

Suggestion -
Now Finished

With (any habit, cigarettes, food as reward, etc.) you're just done and finished. You've moved on and into a forever healthier and better chapter of your life, healthier habits and impulses justifiably guide your way.

Insight –
Releasing Toxicity

Releasing Toxicity as a habit, a mindset, a thought pattern, a pattern of generating emotions and feelings, a memory, a way of life, releasing formerly locked-in unhealthy habits.

Suggestion -
Releasing Toxicity

Right now you are unstoppably free of any and all things toxic in your life, determined, and easily releasing any and all thoughts, feelings, memories, thought patterns, fears, worries and doubts. Now, more correctly, you remain more fluidly and powerfully unstoppable and continually adaptive than ever before, you are thinking correctly and supportively, nurturingly and taking only the very best care of yourself, as your reconfigured and better thoughts, feelings, impulses are now supporting you. Your feelings are pleasant and conducive to a happy life; happy memories. In addition to actively generating a better future life you are re-identified, all life is now supporting you.

Insight –
Harmony Feelings

Actively instilling a sense inner peace and harmony enables inner wisdom to surface and will motivate, allowing your client to do better.

Suggestion –
Harmony Feelings

So relaxed now, you are feeling fine, wonderful, even fantastic. Just as if you've just had a five-hour nap and three solid hours of full body massage; feeling just fine, as your body, emotions, thoughts and memories and feelings, even your spirit, in a new and more powerfully harmonized place of peace, you remain profoundly optimized for success, active, fully functioning harmony, feeling truly and deeply better than wonderful and excellent, on top of your World. Now and forever you are moving into the very best chapter of your life. Rising to the very top, you are thriving and succeeding, forever free of procrastination, activating and living your dreams in harmony, bringing them to life. You are unbeatable and rising to the very top, into the brand-new achieving the very best chapter of your life, which begins unstoppably right now and forever, only getting better, stronger and more and more fluidly adaptive, all working only in your favor, now, always and forever.

Insight –
Sense of Freedom

The world's people seek freedom. Anyone trapped in a habit seeks freedom and release, especially once the habit is recognized as unhealthy or destructive.

Suggestion –
Sense of Freedom

All things once imbalanced are now releasing, ever more completely and actively released and resolved. All things once a hindrance now resolving and ever more completely resolved. So wonderfully, instilled within their place, beneficially turned around in this new chapter, old ways, forever transitioned into assets of empowerment and truest personal freedom as you are and you remain getting forever only better and free, doing better, the very best for yourself. You are loved and supported, breaking through, inspired and limitless, completely freed, released and really wonderful, as never before.

Insight –
Resolution of Stress Blockage

Releasing stress melts the glue holding the habit in its place often releasing the habit freely.

Suggestion –
Resolution of Stress Blockage

All things which once challenged, stressed you out or upset you are now easily handled and even vanquished by you. More effectively, free-flowing, with each and every beat of your heart, and each and every breath you take slowly, stress reduces, results are achieved, the past releases, you are relieved, living better.

Insight –
New Support Structures

Suggesting newer and better self-supporting replacement actions, feelings and behavior patterns to emerge, strengthens both benefit and strengthens connections to a new chapter beginning and forever remaining.

Suggestion –
New Support Structures

Relax now, barrier-free as you liberate new inspirations, allowing brighter, better and even brilliant self-supporting ways of thinking, acting, being and feeling to become a part of who you are. Melt and flow, relax and heal, get now inspired and allow a brilliant and actively productive new and more powerfully real series of new life supporting thoughts, feelings, habits, strategies, support structures and responses to forever emerge from your mind, generating breakthrough success and into all that is your life. A brand-new and better chapter of your life begins unstoppably right now!

Insight –
Known Change

New beginnings are now known to exist and persist, in this brand-new beginning.

Suggestion –
Known Change

In fact, you might just come to now and forever know . . .

Insight –
The Past Now Released

Releasing habits and issues from the past safely back into the past clearly delineates disconnection. The longer ago something happened, perhaps more unimportant and lower impact it becomes and remains.

Suggestion –
The Past Now Released

You know, it's almost funny. You are now and forever so very free now, and free from (name habit - smoking and cigarettes), so firmly entrenched in a happy, healthy and better life, (reinforce any habit - smoke free, cigarette-free), it just simply seems like the previous chapter of your life was yesterday and yesterday now, forever done, really just seems now like a million years ago, so vague, so far away. It feels great to be so free, happy, healthy, content and safe, (name habit – smoke free, cigarette-free). You smile inside and you just know you are contented, serene, happy, very sure and safe.

Insight –
New Beginnings

Instilling a sense of a new beginning, a new start, a new dawn, a new day, a new night, a better chapter, a better life is the restart moment your client is seeking.

Suggestion –
New Beginnings

Your new life now unfolds, in perfect and precise harmony, a new day, a new beginning, a new start, as you just somehow break through here . . .

Insight –
Barrier Reversal and Resolution

In martial arts, reversing the incoming energy of an attack back upon the attacker is a well-known way of stopping most attacks. Reversing back attack energy sends away and disables destructive energy from the one being attacked, eliminating the experience of the attack. Utilizing this reversal technique as suggestion works dramatically.

Suggestion –
Barrier Reversal and Resolution

All "everythings" and "anythings," any and all energies which had ever worked against you are now and forever being turned back upon themselves, to reduce, remove and completely eliminate those negative and destructive energies and limitations. For the greater the challenge, the more reversed remains, while removing, dissolving and eliminating difficulties, ushering in a brand-new and better chapter of your life. As this happens, your possibilities for victories, triumphs, and advances, better habits and better life, expand right now, as you make and take bold strides, opening up your heart and your mind, while magnetizing and liberating only the very best of experiences, breakthroughs, successes and events into your life.

Insight –
Inspirational Success Creation

Structuring suggestions encouraging the subconscious mind to generate inspirational breakthroughs and successes will help self-perpetuate the creation of new habits, and strategies, impulses, habits and actions which drive your client forward toward more surprisingly effective, yet easy, effective results.

Suggestion –
Inspirational Success Creation

Your powerful and adaptive mind is now creating flexible, clever, powerful and even surprisingly and inspired, effective ways to dynamically and easily succeed at this, even anything to which you set your mind. All of this, just getting easier and easier and more adaptive and more powerfully effective for you, in ways known and unknown. You achieve and seize desired results with grace, ease, yet highest, profound, life-improving, life-extending impact.

Insight –
Stepping Forward

Stepping forward from the past into the future is why clients set up their clinical hypnosis session. Often clients are worried the steps they're taking aren't great enough, yet every step is valuable, even a step backwards can lead to further steps forward.

Suggestion - 1
Stepping Forward

It has been said that little steps mean a lot, each step forward a greater stride, this time you are assuredly easily succeeding at . . .

Suggestion - 2
Stepping Forward

Honestly, even if there is a step backwards, more easily now two steps forward.

PART II - ACTIVATING ULTIMATE SUCCESS -

TOOL AND TECHNIQUE UTILIZATION, DEEPENING, AND REINFORCING

IN THIS section I will coordinate previous insights and suggestions into methodologies for deepening, self-perpetuating reinforcement and technique optimization to more fully activate ultimate session success.

As you begin your review of this section, you may find an expanded ways of thinking out of the box, leading to strengthening suggestions via new and inspired insights of your own, setting up and formatting session work to further enhance these many optimized techniques, further ensuring more adaptive and effective suggestions, a stronger session base, while overcoming the natural predilection clients have toward resistance. As we further review these conceptual methods, I hope you will gain further insights into my way of thinking.

Insight –
Resetting

How much easier would it be to help clients improve if we could simply reset a switch, turn a dial, press a button, reset a thermostat or activate a computer of some kind. Often this is how the public thinks hypnotic techniques work. This can be greatly used when suggesting to the subconscious mind.

Suggestion -
Resetting

It's almost as if someone from deep, deep inside of you in this moment has reset a switch, a dial, pressed a button, a thermostat, or a computer of some type, easily allowing you to . . .

Insight –
Foundational Reset

Suggesting it's as if your client's entire life foundation has been reset in a way favorable to habit improvement.

Suggestion - 1
Foundational Reset

In this brand-new chapter of your life, it's almost as if some-one from deep, deep, deepest inside of you has reset a switch, a dial, a thermostat, or computer of some kind, easily allowing improvement, refinement, redefinition, breakthrough, release and relief. Breaking through, you unstoppably achieve any and all goals, now knowing this to be true for you, your better reality, now realized.

Suggestion – 2
Foundational Reset

It is as if someone has reset a switch, a dial, thermostat or a computer from deep within you, resetting you, retuning you, recalibrating you to a better place, your very best now rising to the top, unbeatably.

Insight –
Replacing the Past with Better

It would also be decidedly easier suggesting your client generate life-changing improvements, it's as if any and all challenges that ever stood in their way simply and drained away. Many clients expect thus in this session. Therefore this is essential and effective to use.

Suggestion -
Replacing the Past with Better

It's almost like someone from deep, deep inside of you in this moment has opened a valve from deep, deep inside of you, draining away effectively any and all blockage and resistance energy to ever-evolving, ever-improving, habit breakthrough improvement. In fact, any and all blockage and resistance are now easily being drained away, now drained away and clear. What now instead, forever, fills up this viable and vital space valuably right now, is a beautiful life-supporting energy. An energy of inspired and creative life force, strength, adaptability, self-support, only your very best, acting in your own interest self-supportively, unconditional love, and inner light, vitality and life-force, which easily refills, in endless supply, focusing you, rejuvenating you, and liberating your unbeatable mighty inner hero, unstoppably.

Insight –
Inner Heroic Activation

Inside each of us lives an unstoppable and unbeatable hero is waiting to rise to the top, most especially whenever encountering an emergency or a challenge. Through various life conditioning, whether societal or otherwise, most people are either in denial about this aspect or out of touch. Unleash your client's inner hero and watch amazing things happen.

Suggestion -
Inner Heroic Activation

Your mighty inner hero, a part of you that knows only strength, beyond doubt, remains fearless, courageous and mighty, most especially whenever challenged, has now and forever effectively been activated from deep, deep inside of you right now, powerfully and effectively, creatively and dynamically, most adaptively and effectively, is right now, unbeatably working in your favor to achieve your well-deserved and your very own ultimate success. The part of you that is fully capable of saving children from great danger, or any life-threatening moments is now actively working creatively and adaptively in your favor from deep, deepest inside of you, to break you through, right here and right now, into a brand-new, freer, healthier and better chapter of your life. All of the negative, habitual, stagnating and limiting energies which ever once stood in your way are now cleverly and effectively turned back upon themselves as you adaptively and heroically break through here with ultimate unbeatable, driven success unstoppably.

Insight –
Noticeable Win

Making strides forward and wins more obvious, as issues are resolved and released, generates inspirational success.

Suggestion –
Noticeable Win

It's amazing to notice how easy it is for you to win by releasing and resolving from your life and body, (Name habit – e.g. weight loss- easily dissolving and releasing 23, 24, 26, even 31 pounds).

Insight –
Change as Truth

Foundational shift occurs when change generated now becomes a foundational truth.

Suggestion –
Change as Truth

You smile to yourself and glow from places within, deep inside, knowing the truth of the new day, a new night, life-supporting habits, generating a better life, a substantially, ever improving, better life.

Insight –
Vitally Alive

Tying in personal vitality to improvement, while suggesting a more vitally improved individual, thriving and living, cannot only advance personal improvement, but usher in an entire life upgrade.

Suggestion -
Vitally Alive

You know it feels so great to be feeling so truly wonderful, so vital, so complete, so alive, so completely vitally alive and now thriving, so sure of your life improvement, right here and right now, within such a pivotal and transformational place of your own personal power. So great to be alive, so full of life, and so full of vitality, while you are awake, while you sleep more restfully, even while you were waking up, or even falling asleep, all improvements are just coming together.

Insight –
Automatic Challenge Resolution

Suggesting the subconscious mind automatically and perpetually resolve any possible challenges to forward progress and improvement automatically clears the way to success.

Suggestion -
Automatic Challenge Resolution

In ways both known and unknown, the mightier the challenge ever once experienced, or thought of, in a previous chapter of your life, now done. In this new more self-perfecting chapter of your life, the more formidable and mighty you are and the more empty and forever nothing any former challenge now is, you now rising up, as you self-assuredly stand there proudly and joyously ready to laugh at how effectively easy things have become.

Insight –
Feeling Reinforcement Success

Suggesting feelings which reinforce and support success and improvement makes the changes long-lasting, even permanent.

Suggestion -
Feeling Reinforcement Success

You might even be feeling truly a thousand percent better, certain and sure, ensuring a better life. It's as if you have dynamically succeeded here in the most effective, dramatic and unstoppable of ways, smiling inwardly.

Insight –
Happy Life Extension

Releasing every health-denying habit potentially extends someone's life. When changes are made fluidly and happily, driven as if an individual's life depended on these changes, the more adept your client will be at changing and improving.

Suggestion –
Happy Life Extension

You know you have actually begun anew (~ by forever becoming smoke-free, cigarette-free, breathing easier, feeling happier) right now, as if your life depended on it. As it does and so you have. Free and clear, happy and content, choosing this wonderful choice, you've never felt so good!

Insight –
Smoking Cessation as Life Extension

One of the most valuable sessions any hypnotist can offer someone is to get them free of smoking. As the multiple layers of havoc clear and as their body heals, we potentially extend someone's life, and these beneficial results are invaluable.

Suggestion -
Smoking Cessation as Life Extension

You have already quit smoking as if your life depended on it, because it does, and so now you have, and you successfully remain, both now and forever. You remain unstoppably forever extending your life, and feeling wonderful. Having put your foot down, this forever correct decision, your choice, smoking freedom forever.

Insight –
Self-Perpetuation

Generating self-perpetuating suggestions, effectively adapting past challenges drives forward success and is critical to a new way of taking your hypnotic success to the next level, with each and every client or group with whom you work.

Suggestion -
Self-Perpetuation

Your mind now easily and powerfully generates any and all powerfully effective, self-supporting, progress-creating, perpetual sensations or feelings, pace or plan, you right now or will ever need, to create adaptive and breakthrough success, evermore completely effective, in ways both known or unknown to you.

Insight –
Self-Perpetuating Success

Achieving one's success is a breakthrough, allowing continued self-perpetuation of success improves an entire life. Success building upon success.

Suggestion -
Self-Perpetuating Success

Your always clever and dynamic adaptive mind is now working out beneficial ideas, methods, pathways, solutions, adaptations and improvements to generate success in these highly adaptive, yet effective ways. Success upon success. Most effectively and easily, generating complete and ultimate success, in ways both known and unknown to you, and so it is, and so it remains operating effectively, as therefore you succeed.

Insight –
Limit Resolution

Reducing and completely eliminating past limits which have blocked success or might ever stand in the way of forward progress generates free-flowing success and breakthrough.

Suggestion -
Limit Resolution

All former limitations, now resolved, you now and forever, unlimited.

Insight –
Imagination Generating Success

Every individual we work with has an imagination. Some client's imaginations are more creative and more active than others. Yet unless someone can imagine succeeding, or visualizing success to step into, as a form of self-reunification and success perpetuation, success can remain elusive.

Suggestion -
Imagination Generating Success

You are evermore certain and sure you are succeeding here unbeatably, even if only in your imagination, seeing and experiencing all things in a greater light. Wiser actions and choices now yours, ensuring success. And as everyone knows, your imagination, now thriving and active here, working always in your favor is now making your very best success real and realized.

Insight –
Release and Freedom

Releasing inspirational feelings of breakthrough to generate feelings of freedom is what moving forward to a place of reward is all about.

Suggestion -
Release and Freedom

As you surely feel your breakthrough release, you are released; forever freed, you right now know this to be true.

Insight –
Change as Known Higher Truth

The wisdom of embracing change as a now known higher truth validates improvements and instills a stronger foundation of success.

Suggestion –
Change as Known Higher Truth

Wiser now, all of you now knowing a higher truth, as anything you put your mind to, now more easily than ever before within your grasp. Heroically freed, you now venture ever onward to seize your success and make it one with you, yes, truly making success yours, while enjoying feelings of satisfaction and success, as a deep and true part of you now knows this, making this all your very own. Having done all of the necessary work, succeeding brilliantly. The truth real, this is yours, certain and sure.

Insight –
Inspirational Empowerment as Wisdom and Truth

Asking the careful construction of suggestions, have your client living right now from a greater sense of inspired empowerment, the possibilities, greater sense of knowing, wisdom and a stronger sense of truth can keep them firmly stepping forward and living ever-increasing success, perhaps once a dream, now their new reality.

Suggestion -
Inspirational Empowerment as Truth

Seizing the unstoppable inspiration in this moment while relaxed and effectively empowering yourself, you release and dissolve all and any barriers from your past, consistently flowing ever onward, ever more certain and self-assured, knowing all of this to be true.

Insight –
Activated Determination

By activating a greater sense of determination, more easily challenges are overwhelmed and success is achieved, both long and short-term.

Suggestion -
Activated Determination

For in this new chapter of your life, the more mighty the challenge, the more actively determined you are to achieve your goals unbeatably, effective and adaptable, so it remains and forever is.

Insight –
Mental Resolution

Once any of us has completely made up our mind to succeed, we generally will.

Suggestion -
Mental Resolution

You have set your mind to this, and you, inspired, driven and ever more determined, while doing better and better. For the greater challenge and circumstance, the mightier and more determined, cleverly adaptive and effective, the more driven, heroically inspired you are to break through here unbeatably.

Insight –
Inspirational Best Breakthroughs

Inspired to break through and do better, your clients' drive and determination become more effective and unstoppable.

Suggestion -
Inspirational Best Breakthroughs

Your very best coming up to the surface now, knowing this, all within your grasp, all absolutely and completely within your ability, within your unstoppably determined power to break you through here, activating inspirational breakthroughs, always and forever, and so it is and remains.

Insight –
Life Reset for Health and Abundance

Suggest embracing a life-reset for health and abundance. This insures an alignment towards healthier habits and more abundant life.

Suggestion –
Life Reset for Health and Abundance

Your entire being and life now reset, retuned, recalibrated. In fact all of you actively remains now and forever restoring a better disposition, only getting greater and greater in physical shape, emotional balance and more easily calmer mind. Within this newer, brighter, better, more empowered and inspired point of power you now live your life. You are now readily enjoying all the confidence and stamina to take any and all business or any life issues tuning into a more supportive yet thriving next level, better habits, better life, figuring out and activating new and limitlessly abundant levels of serenity and inner peace.

Insight –
Dissolving Barriers

Dissolving barriers effectively releases impediments towards forward progress.

Suggestion -
Dissolving Barriers

Taking better care of yourself, all things which once stood in your way, are and remain no longer, as you so much easier now overwhelm, setting yourself forever free.

Insight –
Strength Where Weakness Once Was

Fearing past shortfalls effectively empowers shortfalls to return. Reversing shortfalls into motivation and strength effectively frees and unblocks.

Suggestion -
Strength Where Weakness Once Was

Having learned and now doing better, all things once your weakness, now your greatest strengths.

Insight –
Growing Beyond the Past

Anyone's past is simply a memory. In many situations, each of us has the tendency to allow these unbeneficial memories to slow down, create stumbling or completely impede successful progress. Rising above those challenges, now seeing them as learning experiences, which drive progress forward, now more easily releases as a greater sense of wisdom, having been gained by experiencing past issues, now allowing more complete release.

Suggestion -
Growing Beyond the Past

Almost as if you've grown up just a little bit more, having more completely learned and moved on from those experiences, wiser, while gaining greater wisdom and life experience from past lessons, as things of the past now resolved, done and finished, grown up beyond and move forward from, as you, now better and better feeling fine, getting it done, so much more now empowered, inspired, unstoppable, effectively motivated, goals achieved.

Insight –
Tapping into the Inner Greatness

The potential of greatness lies within each of us. Suggesting the greatest aspects of your client rise to the top releases the greatness to do great things.

Suggestion -
Tapping into the Inner Greatness

The greatest aspects of who you are, your inner greatness, now released and liberated into your life, feeling it surface and strengthen you, now breaking you through to do great things, or just instead, simply just breaking through and succeeding more completely right here.

Insight –
Adaptive Self–Mastery

Within each client lies a potential for greatness and mastery over situations once plaguing, standing in their way. They now masterfully rise above.

Suggestion -
Adaptive Self–Mastery

You have masterfully, UNSTOPPABLY and forever entered a brand-new chapter of your life. All of the adjustments necessary, all of the tweaks, any and all things necessary, have been reset, retuned, redefined, and improved in your favor UNSTOPPABLY, as you now and forever know this to be true and real, but because and even in fact it is true from the deepest recesses, from the very best places inside of you. Each and every aspect and area of your life, now working in a greater, higher harmony, as the heroic and mighty inner master of your life, from deepest and most knowing places inside, is now automatically guiding, even allowing this to happen, skillfully adjusting and adapting, only your very best, in the ways which ultimately serve you best and for those that you love the most, most especially yourself, generating success and breakthrough freedoms.

Insight –
Trusting in a Better Tomorrow

Distrusting in future potentials for improvement will potentially short-circuit the result of future improvements coming to be. Trusting future potentials are on the horizon and are rapidly adapting into an individual's life, welcomes the possibility for habit release in life improvement.

Suggestion -
Trusting in a Better Tomorrow

From deep, deep inside, you truly know, yesterday has taken care of you, and tomorrow will do just the same, you trust in this. All of your yesterdays have allowed you to learn or succeed, failure-free, as all of your tomorrows will be just the same.

Insight –
Driven Inspiration

Once your client is feeling a greater sense of inspiration, inspiration is a concept can be used as fuel to drive success.

Suggestion -
Driven Inspiration

Bound and determined, ever actively inspired, motivated, driven inspiration, you rise above and do better, as you do and simply and easily do, of course.

Insight –
Improvement as Known Truth

Skewed sentences intentionally constructed can work covertly to overwhelm resistance both known and unknown within the client. Conceptualizing truth makes a better reality so.

Suggestion -
Improvement as Known Truth

Knowing this now for you, you now know this to be true.

Insight –
Improvement as Truth Now Known

Once a greater truth is understood to be true, the wisdom of this truth generates permanent improvement. This improvement takes place, reflexively, the improvements brought are now known as truth.

Suggestion -
Improvement as Truth Now Known

Now knowing this to be true, your clever and adaptive mind easily works this out for you. All improvements truly unstoppable, easy, completely effective, yet forever.

Insight –
Struggle Release

Struggling drains energy. Releasing the struggle concept ensures successful forward motion toward goal achievement. Many clients have a mindset prone toward struggle, many having used the mindset of struggle conceptualization to ensure blockage and failure, sometimes as a way of skillfully keeping themselves trapped. Often this has to do with a comfort level within stagnating habits. They may be certain of where they are now, and although seeking improvement, unsure of what a future of improvement will look and feel like.

Suggestion -
Struggle Release

Living within this brand-new and better chapter of your life, your correct response to any and all stress or challenge is to relax by deep breathing, slow and steady breath, while flowing forward, right through or even beyond, any and all feelings and actions which have or might have ever once stood in your way. Now in this better place, freedom and release, feeling and healing, just doing simply better.

Insight –
Can and Do

Your client may have tried to improve hundreds of times. Releasing doubt gives permission to improve.

Suggestion -
Can and Do

Yes you can and now so you do.

Insight –
Heroic Breakthrough Generation

Throughout the length of human history, heroes always get

the job done. When your client becomes their own hero, they can effectively become unstoppable.

Suggestion -
Heroic Breakthrough Generation

The heroic and unstoppable part of you, the most powerful, rising-to-the-top aspects are practically super–powered and unbeatably driven, evermore determined to break you through here, realizing complete achievement, now knowing this within, from deepest places, generating a breakthrough inner hero, always getting focused and achieving into a free and forever life.

Insight –
Knowing a Better Truth

All words and sentences are really only communication constructs, expressing something deeper. Getting your clients' wisdom to a place of knowing and better truth, beyond even words, to what these concepts truly mean, instills a greater sense of purpose and direction, ultimately activating goal achievement consciousness.

Suggestion -
Knowing a Better Truth

Actually feeling all of the very best of this and just right now knowing this to be true, beyond what even these words are or may mean, all of you is becoming one with this, right down to the truest levels of healing and knowledge, as truth and fact. A new and better life begins.

Insight –
Foundational Shift Toward Knowing

Once a client knows, comes to understand their life is improving, and all steps are happening actively, passively, or even automatically, they now can come to more fully understand and truly come to know destructive thought and emotional patterns locking in old past habits are now releasing. Building a sense of relief, they can more readily embrace the extension of greater unlimited possibilities now within their grasp.

Suggestion -
Foundational Shift Toward Knowing

You may even be surprised at how much you feel, you think, you know, beyond what even it is you now know. You now know you are completely succeeding. As if all of it happening on its own, finding profound comfort and ever more reliable trust.

Insight –
Emotional Shift Toward Knowing

Balancing and restoring emotions to a place of self-support uses your client's emotional sense of feeling to back up and support improvement.

Suggestion -
Emotional Shift Toward Knowing

Truly in this place of healing, you can actually feel shifts and improvements taking place, now knowing any and all of this to be true, permanently and effectively adaptive for you.

Insight –
Empowerment Confusion Suggestion

This can be powerful. For the resistant client, sometimes using confusion suggestions allow the subconscious mind to get out of its own way and make the improvements in spite of any and all resistant issues.

Suggestion -
Empowerment Confusion Suggestion

You know, you don't know, what it was you think you knew, so now better instead, you now know what it is to know, well now knowing all of this, you simply yet forever now know.

Insight –
Release of Words and Language Pattern Blockage

Beneficially improving internal communication allows and actively promotes improvements, generating the release of the past patterns and habits which stood in their way.

Suggestion -
Release of Words and Language Pattern Blockage

As you enjoy deeper and deepest rest and relaxation here, you activate all the words, thoughts, ideas, concepts, feelings, inspirations and their adaptations beyond whatever these words can simply mean, into greater levels of action and energy, to full effect, more fully achieving, breaking you through and succeeding. Relaxed and comfortable, yet completely driven to transform your life into your desired goals, a more self-perfecting place, happy, healthy, and safe, better impulses and habits as old communication clears, easily achieving any and all goals. For yourself within your life, this you now know.

Insight –
Reorientation Toward *I Can* Thinking

The average person has 50,000 thoughts a day, 75% of which are negative. An average client's subconscious mind will negatively condition a break in forward motion and interrupt success. Reversing this pattern back upon itself liberates creating a sense of freedom. From now on, for every past "I can't succeed" there now becomes an "I can."

Suggestion -
Reorientation Toward *I Can* Thinking

For every I can't there was, is, or may ever have been, turning the page, there is an I can, I will, and right now I do. Proper and effective action equals your well-deserved and wonderful success.

Insight –
Self-Perpetuating Hypnotic Suggestions

Harnessing the power of the subconscious mind to adaptively self-perpetuate the reinforcement of hypnotic suggestions, even adapting them as need be to future challenges. This is taking hypnosis to the next level to ensure success.

Suggestion -
Self-Perpetuating Hypnotic Suggestions

As you relax deeper and further, your now always working-in-your-favor automatic and dynamic subconscious mind, begins to powerfully yet effortlessly, even unnoticeably, work out any and all challenges and issues as they arise automatically, to maximum benefit and effect, both relentlessly and unstoppably, while you are awake, while you are asleep, even while happy, pleasant dreams guide you into resolution and a better night's rest, while skillfully guiding your way into a better tomorrow and life, as you now know your transformation into a better chapter of life and better life-supporting habits to be only actually true and functioning.

Insight –
A Reorientation Towards Empowerment

While growing up, most individuals have not been oriented towards a more fully-functioning empowerment, and grow up feeling powerless. Empowering your client to succeed opens up the universe of possibilities. Activating their subconscious mind to effectively and actively achieving these possibilities empowers ultimate success.

Suggestion -
A Reorientation Towards Empowerment

You might begin to feel a bit unbeatable as you more fully are now driven to ultimate and more self-perfecting success. Your now fully-functioning, working, effectively yet only-in-your-favor subconscious mind, will and must now perpetually work out any and all details to allow you to thrive, while effectively supporting any and all goals you're seeking to achieve to your maximum benefit. In this place, a new and better way of thinking, feeling, living, responding, even existing in this brand-new and better chapter of your life now blossoms, opens, all of the very best now reinforced on each and every heartbeat and breath.

Insight –
Knowing

Knowing improvement is taking place not only makes it easier to accept, but dramatically easier to activate. In a place of knowing success, your session impact becomes more unstoppable and effective.

Suggestion -
Knowing

Already having broken through in this way, you're unbeatable, unstoppable, undeniable and heroically inspired, feeling completely unstoppable in achieving your ultimate goals to generate breakthrough success. Your powerful and automatic mind, activating only your very best, inspired and more easily driven forward, achieving all things unstoppably, leading to a better life. Knowing all of this is in fact to be true, your determination is unlimited, while masterfully achieving breakthrough success. Reset, retuned, recalibrated better thoughts, inspirations and ideas open your mind to inspire everything and anything it takes to honestly activate success in generating breakthroughs, a benefit here, your profoundly better knowing has taken place.

Insight –
Clearing the Way – Challenge Oriented

Releasing the subconscious concept of the problem, and converting the problem concept into a *challenge* makes addressing the challenge and its transformation, more probable, immediate, while generating a sense of rising up to meet and overwhelm said challenge.

Suggestion -
Clearing the Way – Challenge Oriented

In all moments of your life, most especially whenever challenged, your automatic and dynamic, forever now always fully functioning in your favor, your subconscious mind has powerfully and forever cleared the way of challenge orientation. Truly forgiven, fully and forever released problem and struggle orientation, while moving onward into this brand-new and better chapter of your life, where you are and you adaptively create and remain both now and forever problem free, and forever now and always, driven and motivated to create only your very best, *challenge oriented*, ready to rise up to face down any and all challenges, or perhaps instead, just simply creating permanent and long-lasting life improvement in ways most effective, adaptive, effective, and meaningful.

Insight –
Learning or Success

Reducing or eliminating the concept of failure is key. Shifting failure concepts and related fears into either learning or success improves the subconscious process and supports improvement and self-perpetuating refinement.

Suggestion -
Learning or Success - 1

You may just be thinking to yourself, "In my life I am released and failure-free, I either only learn or I succeed; all of my life is a learning experience, forever and always connected to my success."

Suggestion -
Learning or Success - 2

You may even notice yourself perceiving or even knowing the following truth: In this place of true and lasting inspiration, in this brand-new chapter of my life where I now and forever live, I am forever failure free; any and all things I once ever considered a mistake are, now and forever, a learning experience. I embrace all learning to create better impact and success in my better life.

Insight –
Free-Flowing Metaphor

Creating a visual, auditory, or contextual metaphor most people understand forever creates a parallel to that metaphor in terms of individual success and breakthrough patterns.

Suggestion -
Free-Flowing Metaphor

Like a mighty river flowing down the side of the mountain in the spring, you flow over, around, beyond, through, any and all things once considered obstacles, unblocked and free-flowing. Now in this place, you are forever barrier-free, getting where it is you need to be.

And like a boulder in that fast-running stream of water, any and all things which might ever have once been considered adversity, or ever once stood in the way, and now appreciated as having polished you making you better, brighter, shinier, and new. So now and forever, you are forever successfully flowing forward unstoppably while achieving ultimate success and goals, into this brand-new and better chapter of your life.

Insight –
Unstoppable Inspiration

Requesting the subconscious mind to support your vast improvement as a form of unstoppable inspiration supports, generates and drives an engine unstoppable improvement.

Suggestion -
Unstoppable Inspiration

As you relax a deeper and further, further and deeper, it's as if a new energy is around you, keeping you optimistic, clear, focused, a bit more aware and alert appreciating your past, its lessons, and your ability to rise above. But most of all, unstoppably inspired, driven forward, you now are and forever remain heroically unstoppable in your inspiration to succeed, forever freed of the past, doing everything and anything it takes to honestly succeed in breaking through into the kind of a life you now know you deserve and unstoppably and unbeatably create. Resting within this truth, you now find peace.

Insight –
Challenge Resolution

The subconscious mind can be a powerful engine of change. Just as in previous chapters of your client's life, where once subconsciously stuck, so too can that pattern be turned around now in their favor unbeatably.

Suggestion -
Challenge Resolution

Your improvement into this new chapter of your life is ongoing, in all moments, most especially whenever challenged, you now knowingly, and even impulsively, generate better, choosing to either learn or succeed. Any and all challenges, either great or small, known or unknown, automatically resolving and mopping up on their own, breaking you forever and unbeatably through into only your very best. Your best just keeps getting better and better.

Insight –
Unstoppable Intent

Keeping your client motivated and driven toward success, most especially in spite of any arising challenges, can be a critical factor in driving success and breakthrough. Yet if the successes are at hand, within their grasp, and even known, effective action is now taking place adaptively on its own.

Suggestion -
Unstoppable Intent

In this your moment in time, your intent to succeed is both now and forever unstoppable effective action, almost as if you've already achieved success, now at hand, effective action, taking place adaptively on its own, as right now you having made it your own, as your breakthrough success here, completely unstoppable.

Insight –
Overwhelming Challenges with Intent

In challenging situations, either the client will win or their challenge will overwhelm. When beneficial outcomes are permanently sought, it is important for the client to overwhelm the challenge this time and forever, rather than the past now-finished backsliding days of allowing the challenge to overwhelm them. Lessons learned, your client rises up.

Suggestion -
Overwhelming Challenges with Intent

The greater the challenge, the mightier you become, as your automatic mind now works this out unbeatably in your favor, your overwhelming intent to succeed unquestionably overwhelms all challenges, while you are awake, while you are asleep, even while happy pleasant dreams guide your way into a better day, a better night, a better moment called the rest of your life, into the next best chapter of your life, truly knowing this now, you live from this, for you, now knowing this to be true.

Insight –
Point of Power - Present Moment

All transformation and improvement must start in the present moment and continue ever onward into the future, for it to be long lasting, permanent, and forever.

Suggestion -
Point of Power - Present Moment

In this present moment, your power-point of transformational power. For beginning right now for the rest of your life, more perfected and ever-evolving improvements, adaptation, and better life-supporting wisdom begins. Responsibility, drive, determination, dynamic breakthroughs, better more supportive thoughts and feelings, to more completely reshape for the better your life into your now unleashed very best chapter, beginning right now, and only getting better and better over time, on each and every breath and heartbeat, you are forever truly doing only better and better.

Insight –
Releasing Memories of Connected Emotions and Reactions

It's easy to establish habit patterns, keeping oneself trapped, as one reacts to challenges in the same way they always responded. For example, when situation A happens, I react by doing X. The suggestion to release these reactions, helpful in the long-term, will even generate permanent change.

Suggestion -
Releasing Memories of Connected Emotions and Reactions

In this brand-new and better moment of your life, your automatic mind now forgiving, releasing, resolving, evaporating, any and all past connected memories of reactions and emotions which ever drew you back in. For in this place you live in right now, you are forever free.

Insight –
The Last Day

When it's the last time, it's over.

Suggestion -
The Last Day

Your last day of (or hour, minute, moment of –name behavior) now over, done, forward forever and onward, free at last, finished, done, you forever happy, success!

Insight –
Brand-New Chapter

In a brand-new chapter of someone's life, much like a sketch pad, an individual can create, include or even exclude anything they would want from the portrait of their life, which they are now going to create, or re-create. Anything could be included or excluded, items of a life- supporting nature, feelings, habits, ideas, the way they now look, having succeeded, as well as resolving to keep themselves free of all and everything from the past which led them to less beneficial behaviors and habits. In this new landscape, only their brightest and best have room to appear, the past resolving and resolved, supporting them incredibly into the future.

Suggestion -
Brand-New Chapter

As you relax deeper and further, floating into deepest levels of relaxation, you unstoppably begin a brand-new chapter of your life, where you can include and create anything you want or even exclude anything no longer necessary. A place where you now know you are now and forever liberated, reset, re-tuned, re-calibrated, only getting better and better in ways meaningful. In this place you only put your best stuff. You have effectively moved from your now forgiven and released past, having learned and graduated, moving on, while also more completely releasing any and all imbalance and unpleasantness, into the masterpiece chapter of your life, creating and re-creating life-supporting items, feelings, habits, ideas, the way both you and your life now look beginning right now and into the future, better having succeeded, for the rest of your life.

Insight –
Dissolving Limitations

A client's lifetime time can lead to a series of limitation beliefs and actions, keeping them trapped in old behaviors and patterns. A supportive subconscious mind can drive your client forward to a more peaceful, prosperous, and self-supporting life, beyond the session's purpose, generating even greater and more beneficial life-supporting improvements.

Suggestion -
Dissolving Limitations

Relaxing now deeper, feeling free and truly now knowing you are now free forever of past limitations, now dissolving, cleansed, forever washed away, evaporating, melted away, released, even laughable. Completely now knowing you've moved so far forward, you just know you will always create, unstoppably and adaptively generate a greater, grander more life-empowering improvement, getting you forever to where you need to be, in ways both known and unknown. As your now functioning only in your favor, working heroically to your benefit, subconscious mind is evermore effectively balancing this out for you, always by adjusting and refining. Trusting in this fact, you now live from a better truth and knowledge.

Insight –
Maximum Benefit - Both Known and Unknown

With a now empowered subconscious mind working favorably, suggesting improvements to maximum benefit beyond any conscious thinking, in ways affected, both known and unknown, only leads to greater impact and improvement.

Suggestion –
Maximum Benefit - both Known and Unknown

To your maximum benefit, and in ways both known and especially unknown to you, your automatic subconscious mind is now on your side, supporting you, while driven unbeatably to your ultimate success and goal achievement, generating unstoppable and complete beneficial breakthrough results.

Insight –
Actively Regaining Balance

When stumbling occurs, suggesting more rapid rebalancing helps your client get back on track faster and to maximum beneficial effect. For every time they stumble, more adaptively and quickly they respond effectively in centering once again.

Suggestion –
Actively Regaining Balance

Within everyone's life, the possibility of a stumble may occur. In this place, inspired empowerment now actively effective, as you more automatically and adaptively refine your balance, more effectively and quickly, staying and getting back on track, regaining balance and focus, more formidably and favorably succeeding, rebalanced and restored to a maximum habit-improving benefit.

Insight –
Self–Adaptation – Perpetual Effectiveness

The future of hypnotic suggestion involves creating adaptive suggestions which continue to refine and improve, generating perpetual effectiveness, not only in habit resolution, but further overall refinement and improvement for a more beneficial life. All levels of the mind working in harmony to improve.

Suggestion –
Self–Adaptation – Perpetual Effectiveness

As you continue to improve, any and all of this just gets better and easier as time goes on. Your powerful and dynamic mind continues to adapt and generate ever-increasing, greater success perpetually, while you are awake, while you are asleep, and resting, while happy, pleasant dreams, release any and all resistance, to maximum benefit, in ways both known and even unknown to you. Each and every night, you are sleeping deeper, easier, quicker, better, even falling back to sleep sooner achieving more profound rest.

In this more restful place at night, your mind works out to your benefit only your very best, more restfully and deeply, resourcefully, with even greater benefit. Awakening the following day fully ready to take on all challenges, while creating only better habits, within your life improvement. You may even notice yourself smiling more often as you realize the days of struggling from past chapters of your life, now over, as in this place your correct choice, only activating greater levels of success, action, and breakthroughs, more easily knowing, greater benefit and achievement, feeling wonderful, only getting better and better.

Insight –
Inspiration and Optimism

Things being what they are in the world can lead individuals to a place of pessimism, and pessimistic people will generally find reasons and excuses to block success, even actively working against themselves. Inspired clients who are optimistic succeed dramatically most often.

Suggestion –
Inspiration and Optimism

You may just find, enjoying this brand-new and better chapter of your life, better feelings suddenly emerging, even when least expected, almost like a weight has been lifted off you somehow, relief, leaving you feeling unstoppably inspired, and actively optimistic, now knowing better choices result in better outcomes, a greater sense of wisdom makes goal achievement yours.

Insight –
Mighty Inner Hero

Within all of us reside a mighty powerful individual, a hero, the aspect of us who rises up to the top, most especially whenever challenged and find ways to succeed in spite of all thoughts. Anyone reading this has had a moment like this in their lives, yet so many remain in denial of it. Activating your client's inner hero to rise up unbeatably activates the ability to transcend limits, and succeed even in situations which might appear overwhelming.

Suggestion -
Mighty Inner Hero

In this place of deep relaxation and inspiration, your mighty inner hero, your true unbeatable breakthrough winner, who you actually are foundationally, and have always been, now rises to the surface in your life, actively working in your favor, and precise measure, with adept skill and ease, sorting out and working out for you any and all issues to generate a greater sense of active freedom, activating your goals into your reality, as you now know this to be true.

Insight –
Mighty Inner Hero Rising

So always suggest this heroic activation and rise of their mighty inner hero to supportively generate ever more effective improvement, most especially whenever challenged.

Suggestion –
Mighty Inner Hero Rising

Your mighty inner hero, a part of you that knows only strength, beyond doubt, remains fearless, courageous and mighty, has now and forever effectively been activated from deep, deep inside of you right now, powerfully and effectively, creatively and dynamically, most adaptively and is right now unstoppably working in your favor to achieve your well-deserved and your very own ultimate success. The part of you that is fully capable of saving children from great danger, or any other life threatening moments, is now actively working creatively and adaptively in your favor from deep, deep inside of you, to break you through right here and right now into a brand-new, freer and better chapter of your life. All of the negative, habitual, stagnating and limiting energies that once ever blocked you in any way, or ever once stood in your way, are now cleverly and affectively turned back upon themselves as you adaptively and heroically break through here with ultimate unbeatable success unstoppably.

Insight –
Empowerment – Removing Power Blockages

Many clients can be quite clever about blocking forward success, most often on a subconscious basis. Truthfully, your clients may wish to succeed consciously, yet are doomed to failure through life conditioning, keeping themselves trapped in old behaviors and patterns. Who can be more effective at blocking us than ourselves? Dissolving power blockages, effectively overwhelming issues which once stood in their way, generates more powerful improvement.

Suggestion -
Empowerment – Removing Power Blockages

From this moment on, a new and rising sense of inner power is now seen, felt, noticed, fully known to exist within you as you are embracing a higher and more empowering truth, as inspired feelings help un-limit you, driving you forward, as a new sense of a more empowered you, more automatically thriving in successful goal achievement, is now your own, supporting you in every way, physically, mentally, emotionally, and in ways both known and unknown to you, now forward flowing, barrier free, you flow ever onward. In fact, you might just come to feel as if empowered as never before!

Insight –
Activating Internal Power

Opening your client's mind to the possibility of a greater source of internal power and transformation activates wisdom and instills confidence.

Suggestion –
Activating Internal Power

You already have within you all the power, modes, methods, tools and techniques to change and improve anything in your life. Actively working in your favor now, in this moment right now and into your future forever, you set forth into unstoppable action, everything more improving you have already set your mind toward. This power within you now demands improvement, internal power now activated and so passionately creating change, release, relief and improvement. At this point of power, at this pivotal moment in your life, in all moments of your life, your mind now creates changes easily and efficiently, better skills, better habits, better life, and in ways known and unknown, you relax, trust and now know, you effectively accomplish this.

Insight –
Taking Back Power

Many clients speak of living within a feeling of powerlessness, which has become a way of life. If your client is powerful enough to create something, they are powerful enough to create something better. The greater aspects of your client's mind need to take their power back. Every act of feeling powerless takes some degree of power. Once the feeling of powerlessness is reversed, power is taken back, and power directed toward improvement. In this moment your client is and remains empowered to succeed.

Suggestion –
Taking Back Power

In any moment whenever challenged, you stop, deep breathe, relax, and immediately feel a powerful relaxation shift. Within that moment, relaxed, you, now so inspired to step outside the moment, slow and steady soothing breath, brings a rise in life force and greater wisdom, understanding, a greater truth now upon you, more perfectly reconfiguring, while know you are now doing and knowing better. Truly inspired, heroic, relaxed and easily enabled to rise above, mighty, and choosing to do something better, self-respectful and self-loving, always.

Insight –
Vanquishing Fear

It's easy to understand how fears from the past, present, or unknown future can stand in the way of habit release and life improvement. Most often fear is picked up from others as we grow, and past memories, often irrational, come from deep within the subconscious mind.

Suggestion –
Vanquishing Fear

Any old fears are now forever releasing. Fears are like shadows, from within removed by a higher light. In this new and stronger pivotal moment of your life, the light of your life-force shines from within your heart and mind, washing away all shadows, enabling a sense driven inspiration, while you remain forever dynamic and mighty, driven to more unbeatable, better and more unlimited choices, health and life improving actions, habits, reactions, flourish mightily from inside of you. Your light shines bright, washing away all shadows, in a higher light you are so free.

Insight –
Vanquishing Doubt

A key element in blocking one's power is doubt. I have had many clients tell me, "I know this has worked for 12 my friends before my coming here, yet I'm not like them, things don't always work in my favor." A doubtful mindset diminishes long-lasting results. Doubt can be easily overwhelmed by the subconscious when appropriate suggestions are given.

Suggestion –
Vanquishing Doubt

In a greater healing harmony, your habit-improving transition takes place, generating positive forward movement, living within greater trust, transformation, breakthrough, and success, your heroic best driven to ever completing success, now rising within you, as a new and better way of knowing, and living, motivated, while unstoppably persevering, generating ultimate goal achievement.

Insight –
Self–Forgiveness for Release of Critical Self-Judgment

An additional trap blocking progress can be the process of critical self-judgment. Many clients judge themselves harshly, becoming their own harshest critics. In fact, should someone else have treated them as harshly, such a person would quickly be removed from their lives. Yet day-to-day, critical self-judgment impedes habit release and life improvement. Time to dissolve critical self-judgment as a blockage.

Suggestion –
Self–Forgiveness for Release of Critical Self-Judgment

In this new a better place of empowerment, you now knowing better and living better. You allow yourself the adaptive resiliency of learning, rising above, releasing self-judgment, and replacing it better and instead with wisdom, understanding, adaptive resiliency and self-love, effectively succeeding within moving forward, in ways both known and unknown to you, flexibility, while remaining fluid and flexible, guiding your way to greater success, breakthrough, achievement, wisdom and understanding.

Insight –
Redefinition – Problem-Free, Challenge Orientation

A problem by its definition implies struggle, and the possibility of failure. However, most of what people call problems are actually challenges, which once risen up to face, or face down, become issues which can be resolved and learned from. Moving mindsets away from problem thinking and suggesting challenge orientation to your client increases success and effectiveness.

Suggestion –
Redefinition – Problem-Free, Challenge Orientation

In this new and better moment of your life, you are and effectively remain problem free, challenge oriented, easily rising up to meet any and all challenges, for the greater the challenge, the mightier you become, the more effectively adaptive and successful.

Insight –
Achieving Unity - Diffusing Duality
Success versus Failure Issues

In a place of unified improvement, most any improvement is possible. If someone had a dream in which they were walking around on the surface of the sun, from the surface of the sun's point of view, all things are light, shining light, or having a potential for greater light. Scattered thought leads to lack of focus, lack of focus leads to impeded progress. Suggesting the release of failure as a concept and replacing it with the idea of success or learning, allows an individual to succeed, or to learn from stumbling.

Suggestion –
Achieving Unity - Diffusing Duality
Success versus Failure Issues

In this brand-new and better chapter of your life, new ways of thinking and appreciating your life and yourself now seem to be arising in your mind, instilling a sense of strength, harmony, and peace, as you now view your life and yourself in a better way. Released and even laughable right now, the concept of failure, for in this new chapter of your life, all is either success or learning experience, in every moment, you gain, you win, you break through, even thrive and succeed.

Insight –
Fundamentally Transcending the Past

So many clients identify themselves by their past and what they've been through. In reality, they are so much more than that. Rising above the past clears the past so new improvements can be made, embraced, and lived from. Improved self and re-identification more easily takes place.

Suggestion –
Fundamentally Transcending the Past

In this place of inspiration, fundamentally transcending the past, you rise above any and all challenges, as things once considered blockage, they now, so small, insignificant, and so much lesser than you. For in this place, you both now and forever are and remain, rising up, brighter, better, shinier, newer, reset, retuned, recalibrated, thinking better, feeling better, living better, energetically having risen up in a greater truth and a higher wisdom, your best and even better begins and continues long-lasting.

Insight –
Activating Inner Wisdom

Their greatest them, their heroic aspect, the inner wisdom of your client at once rising up in their favor to generate breakthroughs, opens the door to a better day and a better life, a greater them now arising, handling all issues effectively.

Suggestion – 1
Activating Inner Wisdom

In a place of higher inner wisdom and understanding, forever activated, you now reside. As this greater you is now released into the world around you, your very best now coming up to the surface, at your best, more resilient, cleverly adaptable and driven forward to success, while even so much more achieving and unstoppable, handling everything effectively.

Suggestion – 2
Activating Inner Wisdom -

Within these moments right now, activated inner wisdom, more boldly and creatively living within your masterpiece chapter. This is where your now and forever better life begins, your mighty unbeatable inner hero is activated, as if given powerfully effective transformational skills by a wise master of your life, now at your disposal, effectively used. Reflexively knowing automatically what to do next, you always stay on track, bounce back, taking effective steps in effective measure. Just doing so much better now.

Insight –
Automatic Transition

What if all issues were resolving automatically, and completely, free of struggle possibilities and were simply taking place, as if on their own.

Suggestion –
Automatic Transition

You know, somehow it just seems automatic transition and change, in fact all improvements you have set out to unbeatably to effectively generate and create, just seem to be taking place automatically and easily yet powerfully, on their own, almost as if someone from deep, deep inside of you has reset a switch, a dial, a thermostat, or a computer of some kind, as improvements so beneficial and thriving, life improving, just seem to be happening on their own.

Insight –
Stepping Outside the Moment

All too often when challenging situations arise, clients backslide while getting swept up in the moment, resorting to learned reactions such as maladaptive coping behaviors, like smoking, overeating, etc. Stepping outside the moment by briefly detaching, to a greater place of insightful understanding, while remaining clear of being swept up, allows inspired thoughts, effective adaptation and reaction, as the client now does better, making better choices.

Suggestion –
Stepping Outside the Moment

In each and every moment, whenever challenged, you automatically deep breathe, slowly and easily, detach, while now choosing to rise above, become mighty, heroic, inspired, even stepping outside the moment to remember your empowerment, and all things necessary to achieve your goals, precisely, effectively, easily, with skill, and grace. In this place, you live, better love, with ever-increasing self-respect, for whatever the challenge, you now always rise above, stick to your truths, and succeed.

Insight –
Activating Breath to Transform the Moment

One of the easiest ways to step outside the moment is to take a slow and steady breath, detach from the moment, rather than being swept up, and, sharing a better insight, thereby allowing better reaction. When suggested as a subconscious shift, realizations allowing behavior improvements can be utilized for success and habit improvement.

Suggestion – 1
Activating Breath to Transform the Moment

From now on, focusing on your freedom, your inspiration,

and the true fact you now know you are living forever within this brand-new and better functioning, more fully living chapter of your life. In any moment, most especially whenever challenged in any way, you may immediately find somehow, before reacting in an old way, you always now take one slow and steady deep breath, hold it for a moment, releasing it very slowly, and as this happens, a mental shift toward the higher, an inspirational shift in your consciousness knowingly is felt and takes place, stepping outside the old moment into a new better supportive moment, living now better as you are. And in that breath, you transform the moment, better thinking, reflect, and decide to do something better. Being true to yourself, responding better, how great it is to feel and be so free! Forever now, automatic and self-perpetuating improvements taking place, it's just as easy as taking a breath, improving always on each and every breath you take.

Suggestion – 2
Activating Breath to Transform the Moment

In this brand-new and better chapter of your life, your correct response to any and all stress or challenge, is to relax by deep breathing, slow and steady breath, your way right through any and all feelings and actions which ever once stood in your way, feeling, and healing, doing simply better.

Insight –
Rising Above the Moment

Your client is living some moment they have created or are experiencing for perhaps a process of learning. Rising above challenging moments successfully makes this process a continual one and drives success.

Suggestion –
Rising Above the Moment

In this brand-new chapter of your life, most especially whenever stressed or in any way challenged, you will likely find yourself instead responding by taking a slow and steadying deep breath, as a powerful mental and soothing emotional shift occurs, taking you outside and above the moment, generating a new awareness, while instead now, making a better choice, very cleverly and adaptively becoming forever remaining (true to your new way— habit— smoke-free cigarette-free, etc.) while enjoying soothing relaxation breath calming you down, creating your all-important shift, feeling it, even knowing it, better and freedom.

Insight –
Activating Higher Perspectives

From a higher perspective, lesser things are easily resolved, more easily overwhelmed.

Suggestion –
Activating Higher Perspectives

Right now and forever more easily and adaptively, effectively and powerfully, you dynamically rise above any and all situations and challenges presenting themselves both great and small, to become your own great heroic innovator, instituting well-deserved and beneficial change in your life.

Insight –
"Just Imagine"

Everything humans have created, every moment in our lives,

anything improving, takes some level of imagination. Some clients believe they have no imagination, yet all of life from arising in the morning to going to bed at night requires a degree of imagination. Negative mindsets and actions over the years have generated behaviors where truly imagining a better way has become challenging. Activate your client's imagination for automatic beneficial improvements.

Suggestion –
"Just Imagine"

As you relax deeper and further into this better, well-deserved and more appropriately fulfilling chapter of your life, just imagine how great you are at resolving challenges, rising above any and all challenges, and settling into relaxing while remaining in proper perspective, motivated, even dynamically driven, to achieve any and all goals. Just imagine how great it feels, just imagine how easier it's becoming each and every day and night, your thriving success, just imagine how your imagination is now working unbeatably within your favor to generate only your very best, in ways beneficial to yourself and your life.

Insight –
"As If"-

The term, "as if" is loaded with potential power and transformation. "As if" also allows beneficial suggestions to "come in below the radar" with resistant clients.

Suggestion – 1
"As If"-

As if 10, 16, 17 years further down the road, as if someone, somehow automatically, set this improvement into perpetual motion. This is just happening on its own, as if barriers once there, have melted away, as if a mighty river flowing down the side of the mountain in the spring is moving you around, though, over and beyond, to wherever it is you need to finally be on this, truly as if, living and knowing ultimate success.

Suggestion – 2
"As If"-

It's as if all and any of old ways have simply evaporated. As if the old ways have evaporated.

Suggestion – 3
"As If"-

It's as if the clouds from the storm once there have forever drifted away, while right now bright and wonderful Golden-white sunshine were shimmering, inspirationally shining down upon you, bright, or each night, iridescent moonlight embraces and inspires you with a can-do energy, or as if, white puffy-fluffy clouds have serenely and happily filled into that space, inspiring success while fulfilling and supporting you.

Suggestion – 4
"As If"-

In fact, it's as if old issues have been completely forgiven, or as if perhaps instead released, resolved, moved forward from, as if so many decades ago as if brilliance glowing bright within your mind, glowing fully from the inside and the outside, feeling wonderful. I wonder if you have yet realized . . . just to imagine the life you lead freed, now and forever.

Insight –
Almost As If

Activating imagination through the term, "almost as if" allows for adaptive suggestion to continue functioning, generating beneficial breakthroughs.

Suggestion –
Almost As If

Almost as if, having completely resolved any and all issues, and dissolving them forever away in ways known and unknown, your mind is automatically self-reinforcing to maximum benefit any and all of this, you now fully forever know.

Insight –
What If

What if all of these improvements were inevitable?

Suggestion –
What If

What if all you seek to achieve, any and all improvements, were and forever were your inevitable future? As you come to now realize they are!

Insight –
An Assumed Premise as Truth

In college I studied philosophical logic. Although arguing from assumed premise is illogical, when delivering beneficial suggestions for habit improvement, the subconscious mind accepting suggestions non–critically can embrace improvement as automatic and realize a greater truth.

Suggestion –
An Assumed Premise as Truth

In this brand-new beginning of your life, you will find or maybe even better instead, you will just simply notice all improvements happening all around you, as if this is the way it has been your whole life, or instead, just so many years, the more self-perfecting place where you now just currently forever live.

Insight –
False Options

People always love to have options. Clients who have consistently blocked themselves from progress, even *contrarians*, will sometimes prefer hanging on to multiple options. Give them multiple options, but only success-oriented options!

Suggestion – 1
False Options

As you relax deeper and further, floating, drifting, dreaming, deeper and further down, even deeper than ever before, you now knowingly realize, you only will either break through and succeed, or perhaps even better and instead, simply find yourself in some powerful forever moments of life transformation, both happy and free, while forever always remaining, (e.g.: smoke-free cigarette-free; lighter, thinner, healthier, better, more energetic, etc.).

Suggestion – 2
False Options - Smoke Free

You may even find yourself unstoppably smoke free now and for the rest of your life or instead just simply free of cigarettes forever.

Insight –
Excuse Management

Many clients, especially the negatively suggestible client, will use excuses to impede progress. Forgiving and managing excuses resolves blockage.

Suggestion –
Excuse Management

Kicking the old excuses out of your life, you recognize it's time to become true to yourself by becoming forever remaining excuse-free. Forever now stepping up and completely motivated to meet obligations, both great and small within your life, whether the house chores and responsibilities, practically anything which needs doing. Realizing little steps forward each day and night lead to more steps forward throughout the rest of your life. What a great reward! In fact, if excuses are ever made again, you only make them in relation to putting aside the old ways in favor of these new healthier, fulfilling and effective ones, actively bringing your goals achievably into your life, while completely releasing, relieving, forgiving, letting go of, and being done with, growing up and beyond, any and all old thoughts, feelings, ideas, memories or anything present or within the past, emotions, or anything in your life, either known or unknown to you. Now being completely forgiven and released, grown up beyond, let go of, evaporated, dissolved, released, relieved yourself of any areas which have ever stood in your way, completely dissolving these right now. Releasing blockages from the past, even emotional sympathy. Completely within this new and energetically motivated, yet unstoppable chapter, generating your well-deserved masterpiece chapter of your life and body coming on. You are now forgiving, releasing, resolving, and even dissolving, moving forward from and away from, while cleverly relaxing through areas now finished, finding more joy in who you are as a human being, resolved to be living only your very best.

Suggestion – 2
False Options

In this moment you will find you only break through and succeed, or perhaps simply and instead, step-by-step, become free of [name habit] . . . living your dreams and generating only your very best.

Insight –
Complete Destiny

In movies, and in literature, the concept of one's destiny is often mentioned. What if it were suggested that your client life's destiny would be multiple beneficial upgrades and improvements, an ever–evolvement toward continual improvement?

Suggestion –
Complete Destiny

You've always known the old days and the unpleasant ways would soon be over. Whether it's right now, with some moment released forever into the past, you now embrace a destiny of higher wisdom, better behavior, and the release of the old ways, feeling completely relieved, supported, doing differently, living differently, behaving differently with a greater sense of inspirational empowerment and inner and outer peace now your own, free of . . . [any and all desire to smoke anything whatsoever; old ways of eating that no longer support you and your log-term health, forever boring and even silly; giving your power away to stressful situations and circumstances, now more empowered within yourself to rise above, etc.]

Insight –
Time Travel Backward – Issues Never Existed

What if earlier in life other choices have been made, and unhealthy habits were never established in the first place?

Suggestion –
Time Travel Backward –Issues Never Existed

As you relax deeper and further, it's almost as if you would be or are moving backward in time, seeing yourself at an earlier age, seeing yourself at the age of X [any age before the challenge behavior became a part of their lives]. In that moment, at that forever moment, a pivotal point of power, where you put your foot down and made a very strong decision, so certain, facing a choice, having made a better choice instead. So even when you were 12, 13, 14, 15, 16, 18, or 21, and beyond, it's almost as if you always were and you remained, [smoke-free cigarette-free; lighter, thinner, healthier, better; etc.]

Insight –
Time Travel Forward –Issues Never Existed

What if at some future time all of this work has already been done? What if all these improvements have remained successful and standing on their own for many years?

Suggestion –
Time Travel Forward – Issues Never Existed

It's almost as if within your heroic and unbeatable focus, adaptive and strategic effect has been generating release, release, and forgiveness of the past, rising above, achieving wisdom, action and improvement, to ultimate beneficial success, actually or almost like you have been [smoke-free, cigarette-free, for 14, 16, 17 years, each and every day and night, as if you've succeeded all those years each and every day of freedom, habit -- smoking so far in the past; better eating habits, filling up sooner], the past ways forever done, finished, even laughable.

Insight –
Laughing at what was Once the Monster

It is difficult to be intimidated by something laughable.

Suggestion –
Laughing at what was Once the Monster

The greater the challenge, the more calm, relaxed and focused you become; knowing your empowerment, mighty inner wisdom, life-force and strength make your past and any and even all of its most challenging moment, so easily released and forgiven, so powerfully risen above, challenges now resolved and resolving, practically laughable. Having moved on, feeling so wonderful, it's thrilling to succeed.

Insight –
Assets Rather than Deficits

A lifetime of negatively directed thinking, actions, habits, even reactions, lead many to focus on deficits and shadows rather than strengths and the light of inner wisdom.

Suggestion –
Assets Rather than Deficits

Whatever any challenge in the past was, you now recognize and appreciate the true fact you have always survived, but even better right now within this ever-improving chapter of your life, you are fully choosing to thrive, choosing to live, you are doing everything and anything it honestly takes to break through and thrive, effactually step-by-step to ultimate success, activating inner power and your very best assets, achieving your goal unbeatably.

Insight –
Love as an Unstoppable Force

In clinical sessions, the love one has for family members, children, even themselves, can be used as fuel to instill long-lasting change, unbeneficial habit release and lifelong improvement.

Suggestion – 1
Love as an Unstoppable Force

In this new and better chapter of your life, you remain loving yourself better, just as you love your loved ones. In all things great and small, you are doing better, feeling better while rising above any and all challenges more easily. For in this place you remain loving yourself enough and even better and beyond, while generating wisdom and compassion for even yourself, to stay free and liberated from the past into the better. Forever through your self-love, you effectively get to where you need to be and to forever thrive in this brand-new and forever better chapter of your life, always moving forward, breaking through unbeatably.

Suggestion – 2
Love as an Unstoppable Force

As you would do almost anything to better love and protect your children, so too does your automatic mind now focus, and actively work out and appreciate loving yourself enough to improve, release the past, rising up to better love and protect yourself, effectively following through to break through ultimate success, more motivated and empowered, breaking through into achievement of any and all goals, both great and small, while activating limitless success in any and all things you seek to achieve most especially. . .

Insight –
Better Self-Appreciation and Self-Respect

Many habits have been picked up and instilled over the years when self-appreciation, and self-respect have been at low levels.

Instilling greater self-appreciation and self-respect can generate abundant improvements.

Suggestion –
Better Self-Appreciation and Self-Respect

As you now have come into your own power, achieving knowingly your own success, you instill a better sense of self-appreciation, loving self-respect, enough to now know better, actually choosing better, behaving better, succeeding better, achieving and thriving as you have unbeatably stepped out to knowingly do, as you step forward to generate improvement, moving only forward as better steps forward yielding better results, more easily yet permanently achieved.

Insight –
Shining Light

The light of wisdom often vanquishes the shadows of unbeneficial behavior.

Suggestion –
Shining Light

Living in the light of the better day, you remain living in the power of this better moment, sensing, even feeling the shift, as your automatic mind now easily vanquishes any and all shadows from the past within the higher light of true, effective wisdom, creating a dynamic and beneficial shift to where it is you truly need to be. Right now healthy, happy, safe, re-identified, doing and acting better, while always releasing, forgiving, gaining understanding and wisdom, yet choosing to learn better and achieve more, you adaptively and cleverly succeed in a place of higher understanding and higher light, re-identified better, enlightenment and freedom, now and forever yours.

Insight –
Internal Communication Change

Long lasting improvements take place and remain better when internal communication is improved to your client's benefit.

Suggestion –
Internal Communication Change

You may even find yourself thinking all of the following personal and profound now known inspired ideas as a fact, foundational life-truths [name habit – I am so happy to have kicked cigarettes out of my life, what a relief! My health is better, I can breathe again, it's easy, I feel wonderful; eating better food makes me feel wonderful, and I am happy I made the all those necessary changes, I love feeling lighter and better . . .]

Insight –
Eternal and Profound Trust

An enabled trust in the process of improvement reliably and effectively working in your client's favor, perpetually keeps the process of habit release and life-improvement flowing.

Suggestion –
Eternal and Profound Trust

In this brand-new and better chapter of your life, you realize just as the sun rises each morning and sets each night, so too has today taken care of you, just as every yesterday and tomorrow will do so as well. In this profound place of transformational healing called your brand-new and better life chapter, you now more and more each day and night, come to recognize your life as a series of understandings, lessons, wisdom gained, while knowing from places deepest within your life, your world, even your universe, in this new place, evermore supportive, eternal and profound trust. As you relax, barrier-free flowing forward, new and better more supportive thoughts, feelings, ideas, wisdom, understandings, guide your way into a more joyous and success-inspiring life experience.

Insight –
Action Orientation – Dissolving Procrastination

As often excuses have kept your client locked in a particular behavior pattern, which has now become a way of life, and a certain level of comfort, keeping your client motivated through an action orientation will dissolve many procrastination issues.

Suggestion –
Action Orientation – Dissolving Procrastination

Stepping up to seize the moment in your life, you truly come to enjoyably unwind and look forward to reinforcing your hypnosis each and every night on your own, always with deeper relaxation, yet better results, truly looking forward to your time, ever more completely enjoying experience of deep relaxation, as you ever-increasingly and effortlessly generate wonderful success, slipping into hypnosis deeper, easier quicker and better, generating better than wonderful results always.

Insight –
Draining Away Disharmony and Imbalance

Dissolve away the limitations imposed by disharmony and imbalance, replacing it with a sense of harmony and balance.

Suggestion –
Draining Away Disharmony and Imbalance

It's almost like someone from deep, deep inside of you in this moment, has opened a valve from deep, deep inside of you, draining away effectively any and all blockage and negativity energy. In fact, any and all shortfalls, disharmony and imbalances are now easily been drained away. What fills up that space right now, is a beneficial and well-deserved, beautiful energy, an energy of inspired and creative life-force, strength, skillful adaptability, unconditional love, and inner light, which easily refills, a higher and greater harmony and sense of balance, in endless supply, focusing you, rejuvenating you, and liberating your unbeatable mighty inner hero unstoppably, success as if now yours.

Insight –
Release Generates Relief

Releasing old habits and behaviors brings with it the reward of a sense of relief and the possibilities for better.

Suggestion –
Release Generates Relief

Your effective and adaptively working in your favor active mind now easily and powerfully generates any and all powerfully effective sensation or feeling, pace or plan, you now or will ever need to create adaptive and breakthrough success, putting down past burdens. Right now lighter and feeling free, releasing and relieved, in ways both known and unknown to you, ahh, what a relief.

Insight –
Purposely Driving Forward Success

Suggesting forward progress brings greater beneficial rewards.

Suggestion –
Purposely Driving Forward Success

For the mightier the challenge you ever once had, in a previous chapter of your life, you truly come to know it's both now and forever done, released, and forgiven. However it once was, in this new chapter of your life, the more formidable and mighty you are and the more empty and nothing that former challenge now is, as you self-assuredly stand there proudly and laugh at how easy the past is released and how much better things have become. So much more effective you are and you remain.

Insight –
Knowing and Living from a Higher Truth

In a higher place of wisdom, resides higher truth and a greater sense of knowing the process remains continuing beneficially.

Suggestion –
Knowing and Living from a Higher Truth

All of you is now knowing, truly living from a higher truth, as anything you put your mind to, now more easily than ever before within your grasp, activated into the world around you. Heroically freed, you now venture ever-onward to seize your success and make it one with you, feeling and knowing, making success yours, while enjoying feelings of satisfaction and success, as a deep and true part of you now knows this and makes this all your very own. Doing and having done all of the necessary work, continuing to succeed brilliantly. This truth real, this is yours, certain and sure.

Insight –
Succeeding As If Life Depended On These Changes

Instilling a sense of success, as if these changes have your client's life depending upon them, activates the sense of self-preservation, and therefore motivation to achieve long-lasting success. In fact, self- destructive habits are standing in the way of your client's healthier and longer life.

Suggestion –
Succeeding As If Life Depended On These Changes

You quit smoking right now as if your life depended on it. Free and clear, happy and content, you've never felt so good!

Insight –
Complete Life Reset

How easy it would be if people came with a reset switch. Why not suggest a complete life reset?

Suggestion -
Complete Life Reset

As you now smile because you know, any and all resistance blockages dissolving, the more you once resisted improvements in the past, the more this right now is taking place right now, free of resistance, actually a shift is taking place, your complete life-reset. You now know this to be true, you have cleverly reversed the past back upon self, and as it has, doing better and released, feeling supported and fine, you are fully functional and reset, truly free.

Insight –
Life Reset to Truly Release the Past

The concept of resetting one's life can also be used to release the past as the past is merely a story and memory a client is reinforcing, to keep a habit going.

Suggestion –
Life Reset to Truly Release the Past

You may even come to realize your life has been completely reset in your favor. In this place of deep rest, relaxation and inspiration, you know it's almost as if someone has actively reset a switch, a dial, thermostat, or computer of some kind, easily allowing you to release the past and any and all of its blockages, ever-now dissolving and dissolved completely, while generating more optimal beneficial outcomes for your future and most especially your point of power, which is right now.

Insight –
Head Nodding as Reinforcement

An average person nods or shakes their head dozens if not hundreds of times a day. Most of us don't even realize we're doing it as we speak or listen. Connecting this motion as reinforcement will only have beneficial improvements self-perpetuating.

Suggestion –
Head Nodding as Reinforcement

Nodding your head yes simply because you now know it's true and every time you nod your head yes to anything in the future, only when appropriate, you smile inwardly, sometimes even laugh while knowing an ultimate truth of a better goal-achieving life, or instead simply realizing your breakthroughs and successes. Freed from the past and anything to do with past chapters in moments when you [name habit]. Every time you nod your head "yes" when appropriate, or shake your head no to the unpleasantness of the past, realizing your own personal heroic inspiration and better self-appreciation, you are smiling inwardly knowing a greater truth, the past is now done and you have moved on forward, and upward experiencing freedom and truly better, better habits and life, self-supporting in joy and self-appreciation.

Insight –
A Subconscious Yes to Their Very Best

Asking your client *nod their head yes while in hypnosis* is asking your client's subconscious mind to come to the wisdom of full agreement by all necessary to generate improvement. Once the subconscious mind this time, is now working in their favor, they can become an unstoppable force.

Suggestion –
A Subconscious Yes to Their Very Best

(While they are deeply hypnotized near sessions end) Nod your head for me because you now and forever truly know that you've forever relaxed your way into a brand-new and better chapter of your life and really know any and all of this is true. You effectively are creating benefit, even adapting to generate even greater benefits both now and throughout the future, always. *(Wait for their affirmative nod and continue).*

Insight –
Heartbeat and Breathing as Reinforcement

Every living client has a heartbeat and needs to breathe. As if these are automatic processes of the autonomic nervous system, they're essentially useful as subconscious reinforcements for session breakthrough success.

Suggestion –
Heartbeat and Breathing as Reinforcement

With each and every breath you take, and with each and every beat of your heart, you are powerfully liberating the feelings, energy, actions, habits, reactions, improvements and sensations associated with these following thoughts, ideas and concepts into a vital and profoundly true, reconditioning and redefinition of who you are, where you live from, how you respond and whom you now grow forever to be into your life:

you are feeling wonderful and forever improving by becoming *(name the feelings, actions and reactions you wish to instill).*

Insight –
Covert Confusion

The following suggestions below can be powerful. Bypassing critical resistance, these are a part of every clinical session I do. It brings beneficial improvement to a place of greater knowing.

Suggestion –
Covert Confusion

You know, you don't know, what it was you think you knew, so now, even better instead, you now know what it is to know, well now knowing all of this, you now know.

Suggestion –
Covert Confusion - 2

Knowing this now for you, you now know this to be true.

Insight –
Turning Off Struggle

Resolving to release struggle as a concept opens your client to improvements, struggle-free.

Suggestion –
Turning Off Struggle

The days of mulling over ideas of limitation and struggling are finally over, finished, done, outgrown, now powerfully and pleasantly forgiven and released into the past chapter of your life. You, just now, moving on. Should you ever think about them again, you will smile to yourself warmly, feeling a warm heart, and more advancing better knowing mind, in glowing knowing wisdom you have outgrown and risen above these things, better habits and life now yours, so much better you are and you remain, having moved on.

Insight –
Truism

Paralleling a truism into suggestion releases resistance, and promotes unconditional acceptance, as benefit takes place.

Suggestion –
Truism

Just as the Sun comes up in the morning shining a higher light, and just as the Sun sets in the evening, and just as the stars shine bright at night, and as this world moves around the sun, so to do you eternally enrich yourself bringing only your very best while improving beneficially. Now knowing this to be true for you, you break through free of old habits, and release [name old habit]. Truly now within your life, your world, your universe, inside and out shining bright, feeling serene, as profound improvements are taking place, in knowing glowing wisdom of success you now live.

Insight –
Strategies For Success Automatically Formulate

As the subconscious mind is now activated to generate

improvement, new strategies for success will automatically formulate. Much in the way past ways of thinking automatically generated shortfall excuses, so too now in this new chapter success becomes theirs, struggle- free, even automatically.

Suggestion –
Strategies For Success Automatically Formulate

Whether you realize it or not, your automatic and dynamic mind, working profoundly now within your favor, is generating and creating completely effective, well-placed, carefully constructed even amazing improvements, strategies for success which automatically formulate, which although at first not immediately noticed, are in effect and making you feel wonderful, each of these may even surprise you.

Insight –
Days of Living

Your client's days of living more beneficially are at hand, living a better life. Beyond surviving there is simply living.

Suggestion –
Days of Living

In this new and better place, you are somehow always getting to, yet somehow actually have truly arrived, beyond survival, forever better learning to absolutely live and thrive, goal realization achieves better days of living, better life.

Insight –
Serenity and Relaxation as Reinforcement

While an individual is hypnotized they are most often feeling serene and relaxed. These too can be suggested as reinforcement.

Suggestion –
Serenity and Relaxation as Reinforcement

You find within your mind, your world and your life, in this brand-new and forever place, a more restful, serene, stress-free you thriving, a place within you almost contemplative. Your automatic mind so relaxed, yet keyed and attuned, more restful and more rested, reinforcing, automatically more easily able to skillfully work out all things to your benefit with ease, masterfully, keeping you free of old ways while keeping you safe, calm, focused, liberated from the past, better inside and out, firmly and keenly, serenely into the new and better.

Insight –
Laughter as Reinforcement

Scientific studies have shown laughter reduces stress, increases longevity, boosts the immune system, and increases intelligence. The average child can laugh hundreds of times throughout the day, the average adult about six times per a day. Freeing up laughter lightens the mood, and releases negativity mindsets. So suggesting laughter as reinforcement enhances success and can improve your client's life dramatically.

Suggestion –
Laughter as Reinforcement

You will come to know (a color, an item, like a wrist-watch, a ring, a phone, etc.) X - this X is going to become more obvious, more dynamic and inspiring to you than you can even imagine, almost like it's jumping out at you, right into your face, right into your eyes, and whenever appropriate, always making you smile, sometimes even giggle and sometimes even laugh really, really hard, just like a little kid. It is going to seem more soothing, inspiring, more relaxing and more unstoppably inspiring to you, almost as if it's jumping out at you, right into your face, right into your eyes, and only when appropriate, funnier and funnier. Each and every time you are going to be more inspired and unstoppably determined to effectively and adaptively achieve your goal of [becoming remaining smoke-free cigarette-free, lighter and thinner, healthier and better; etc.]. As you notice this remarkable X, it inspires you to be more successful in all that you want to accomplish, wish to accomplish, can, will and in fact do unstoppably, and effectively accomplish, more relaxed, inspired, creatively determined and unstoppably successful than ever before.

Insight –
Consistent Subconscious Adaptation for Reinforcement

There are a wide variety of issues which can arise, sometimes surprisingly and unexpectedly, which might interfere with client's success. Consistent subconscious adaptation as a reinforcement modality will effectively allow your client to succeed even in unexpected moments.

Suggestion –
Consistent Subconscious Adaptation for Reinforcement

As only your very best is rising to the top, now unbeatably for you, in this brand-new and better self-fulfilling empowerment moment of your life, in ways known but moreover generally unknown to you, your automatic and dynamically powerful subconscious mind is now favorably and consistently refining even adapting any and all aspects necessary to keep you happy, safe, while ever more completely achieving your goals, remaining peaceful and even serene, while powerfully knowing you are always automatically working out everything, anything to achieve maximum benefit and success in ways now unbeatable, this now you know profoundly.

Insight –
Reinforcing Inspired Greatness

Building upon inspiration inspires further.

Suggestion –
Reinforcing Inspired Greatness

All of the inspirational energy of the greatest aspects of yourself or other people you've observed now yours, is now rising up unbeatably to solve, resolve, the past as move you forward only as your goal achievement is at hand. You now make any and all of this as your very own, knowing this both in heart and mind. Most especially whenever challenged in any way, only your very best rises energetically and unbeatably to the top, instantly reinforcing your very best, improving all you seek, new ways, better habits, better ideas, and inspirational greatness for you now are knowing better. You now live better, in this new place, more free, thriving and inspired, and enabled to achieve your goal, any goal, for in this place where you now and forever live, all issues resolving, freer, always better achieving.

Insight –
Automatically Overwhelm All Past Issues

Far too often, your client has felt overwhelmed. Isn't it time that they become the overwhelming force?

Suggestion –
Automatically Overwhelm All Past Issues

As you now have come to understand, recognize, realize or somehow instead truly understand all of this as a new foundation, or moreover even better know, a new sense within you has awoken, a boundless energy of a more felt and complete inspiration, a sense of driven-forward determination active, which supports you, as you are now more completely enabled to roll over in order to automatically overwhelm any and all past challenges or frictional moments from the past, as truly courageous and inspired, even driven, all of past blockages now seem to be dissolving and melting, as feelings or even past memories so very resolved, so very solved, so risen above, so overwhelmed, as you now, the mighty one, so forever empowered and inspired. Your forward movement toward your goals, habitual improvements and your freedom, the choice you lovingly give yourself, living from and now and forever know.

Insight –
Expectation - Being the Miracle

Utilizing your client expectations to improve can work miracles.

Suggestion –
Expectation - Being the Miracle

As many who have come for hypnosis generally break through and succeed, the profound improvement and change you look forward to, simply now even as you exhale, has somehow become your own, and eternal part of you. With each and every breath you take and with each and every beat of your heart, is as if the breath is further ushering you into your life full of profound and effective improvements you once sought, even the miracle of complete freedom and change, which is now your own. Your creative mind, with every thought, makes this ever more so.

Insight –
In Spite of and Because of

Utilizing past moments of blockage, now turned around into beneficial support, as if it's happening on its own automatically.

Suggestion –
In Spite of and Because of

You succeed here, in powerful ways, which seem to be slipping through into the reality around you, in spite of, and even because of, times in the past you once blocked yourself. In this place, more powerful your resistance once was, the more you succeed.

Insight –
This in Fact is True – Not Because I Say So

Regardless of the opinion, improvements are simply happening.

Suggestion –
This in Fact is True – Not Because I Say So

Any and all of the beneficial changes are in fact true, as you now know them to be, not because I say so, but rather instead and because they just seem to be happening to your well-deserved, more limitless benefit on your own, in spite of or because of any resistance past, present, or future. Out of your own way once and for all you are and you remain, achieving beneficial success.

Insight –
Blockage Dissolving, Generating Release

Freedom from blockage frees your client to move forward.

Suggestion –
Blockage Dissolving, Generating Release

You have already, creatively and effectively, in ways automatic and meaningful, as you relax deeply within into yourself and into your life, effectively and adaptively, while forgiving, releasing, evaporating and dissolving any and all old habits, actions, reactions, imprints, while powerfully reconfiguring, adopting and adapting new and better ways of living, thriving, and succeeding, rising above any and all past challenges. You are more effectively dissolving blockages and generating effective release.

Insight –
Blockages Become Support

Utilizing blockages to be a means of self-support, convert blockages into something useful.

Suggestion –
Blockages Become Support

Any and all thoughts, feelings, issues, habits or actions once a hindrance, now become a means of support, turned around back from the past, upon themselves, as they collapse, you are better supported, completely free while succeeding beautifully, smiling inwardly.

<u>Insight – </u>

Establishing a New Foundation – Self-Motivation

Build a better foundation, a new life structure flourishes.

Suggestion –
Establishing a New Foundation - Self-Motivation

Self-assured and self-reassuring, beyond even what these words mean into a more meaningful and powerful place of pivotal improvement and profound change, you forever effectively remain. The imbalances of the past now reversed back upon themselves, collapsing themselves, in a viable truth is your strength, your change, your improvement. In free-flowing adaptive wisdom, your profoundest truth. This wisdom is giving your life and yourself new meaning to be and forever only remain at your very best.

Insight –
Forgiveness Motivation – Bringing Freedom

Forgiveness as a force can be utilized to guide forward motion, motivate, and enhance a greater sense of welcomed freedom.

Suggestion –
Forgiveness Motivation – Bringing Freedom

Your unconditional, absolute and complete forgiveness paves the road to a healthier life, better lived, filled with enjoyable freedom, so well deserved, alleviating imbalanced connections to the past, so you now know, you create this, making it so.

Insight –
Loving Enrichment

Loving themselves better, your client's life improves and enriches.

Suggestion –
Loving Enrichment

Opening your heart to yourself more completely, self lovingly, your heart now more open to share your brightest, your best, and other aspects of the richness which is you, in the real and most truest sense of the word, your personal enrichment, freedom and goals achieved, now yours.

PART III–
SESSION CONCLUSION -
BEFORE CONCLUDING THE HYPNOTIC SESSION

IN THIS next section, I want to share some ideas how to make your hypnosis session work more intensely and last even better.

Insight –
Using the Term "When Appropriate"

I've also found it very important to use the words "when appropriate." As you read ahead here and the various examples, it is important to keep focus on the idea that these not ever get out of control.

Suggestion -

You will find yourself more aware of supporting sounds and colors, feeling relaxed and happy, smiling and ready to laugh, in situations supportive, but only when appropriate.

Invaluable Insight –
Instant Reinforcement Triggers

I use instant reinforcement triggers at the end of every hypnosis session/procedure I host—key words or phrases which will instantly activate session impact and habit improvement. I find these invaluable for instant reinforcement and self-perpetuation of various suggestions I am delivering.

Instant reinforcement triggers can be behavioral, visual, auditory and environmental, to name just a few.

I also enjoy using behaviors and environmental factors to reinforce my work. Yet another inside secret to self-perpetuating suggestion and reinforcement.

Insight -
Head Nodding as Reinforcement

The average person nods their head yes or shakes their head no at least dozens of times each day. The movement of the head and neck takes place throughout conversations automatically, as most individuals remain completely unaware they're communicating in this way while speaking.

Suggestion –
Head Nodding as Reinforcement

Nodding your head yes simply because you now know it's true and every time you nod your head yes to anything in the future, only when appropriate, you smile inwardly, sometimes even laugh, while knowing an ultimate truth of a better goal-achieving life, or instead simply realizing your breakthroughs and successes, freed from the past and anything to do with past chapters in moments when you . . . Every time you nod your head "yes" when appropriate, or shake your head no to the unpleasantness of the past, realizing your own personal heroic inspiration and better self-appreciation, you are smiling inwardly knowing a greater truth, the past is now done and you have moved on forward, and upward, experiencing freedom and truly better.

Insight –
Getting Subconscious Agreement - A Subconscious Yes to Their Very Best
Communicating Directly with the Subconscious Mind

There is an amazing skill we can utilize as hypnotists for achieving results. Asking the subconscious mind for agreement with our suggestions while the client is deep in hypnotic trance. It's as simple as having them nod their head yes. As a client is deeply hypnotized, the subconscious mind is responding to you, agreeing with you and now part of the team, on your client-side this time, working with them, creating breakthroughs.

Suggestion –
Getting Subconscious Agreement

(While they are deeply hypnotized near sessions' end) Nod your head yes for me because you now and forever truly know that you've forever relaxed your way into a brand-new and better chapter of your life and really know that any and all of this is true, creating benefit, even adapting to generate even greater benefit, both now and throughout the future, always. *(Wait for their affirmative nod and continue).*

Life Story –

I did hosted workshops years ago in Manhattan for a company called *The Learning Annex*. I was teaching a class of self-hypnosis and meditation. One particular night, each time I attempted to record the group meditation and hypnosis, there was a great deal of commotion taking place across the street. There were loud sirens, from what seemed to be ambulances, fire trucks and police vehicles.

During the lecture portion of the class, noise outside was nonexistent.

Yet when I began to once again perform a group exercise, once again the sirens began and continued.

Many of the people attending wanted to buy copies of these recordings. And when I suggested they purchase recordings from the previous month's workshop, as those recordings did not have background sounds of sirens, each person insisted upon purchasing the copies recorded that night.

When I asked why each of them responded, much to my surprise, "This is Manhattan, we can't sleep unless we hear that stuff." I sold a lot of those recordings. I've since come to use noises from outside as reinforcement, and have come to realize: to let nothing stand in your way when working. Even the sound of a mobile phone can be used to reinforce success.

Insight –
Sound Trigger –Sounds from the Entire World Working to Support Improvements

Suggesting to your client the whole world and all that is your life is supporting this transformational improvement, releasing habits of the past, once destructive, including any and all thoughts, ideas, feelings, as right now a greater potential and more unlimited transformation yields only beneficial improvement, in ways profound.

Suggestion –
Sound Trigger

As you now relax deeper, you now know the whole world works to support you in this, the world and life on your side. You will even find telephone noises of any type and sounds from outside, like car horns, sirens, car alarms, barking dogs, planes flying by, adults having a conversation somewhere off in the distance, children playing nearby making noise, and other sounds instantly reinforce all suggestions, all improvements, even clever adaptation of suggestions to keep you completely clear and confident in the success you now achieve, unstoppably and unbeatably. Any time you hear these sounds or just any of them, instantly reinforce a smoke-free, cigarette-free, you are lighter, thinner, healthier, and better you, are you who is able to sleep beneath those noises, peacefully every single night.

PART IV -
MOST REQUESTED
HYPNOSIS ISSUES AND
POWER BONUS SESSIONS

THROUGHOUT THE course of my career my top seven private sessions remain:

- Smoking Cessation

- Weight Reduction

- Stress Management

- Better Sleep/Better Rest

- Freedom from a Fear

- Better Memory/Better Recall/Learning Enhancement

- Surviving a Breakup/Divorce.

Statistically hypnosis remains way out in front for effective habit improvement, when addressing any of the above challenges.

Professional Insights –
Smoking Cessation Insights

All too often the general public refers to smoking as an addiction. Technically it seems to be more of a compulsion. What many people don't realize is nicotine is used industrially as an insecticide!

A habitual smoker has learned to smoke subconsciously. Even if they have decided to quit smoking, whenever stressed or as challenging situations arise, a person who has learned to smoke reactively is often finishing a cigarette before they consciously realize that they had smoked a cigarette, as their smoking process has become a subconscious one.

If you consider a non-smoker who is beginning to start the habit, a great many aspects go into smoking and cigarettes. First, purchasing ever more expensive cigarettes. Then finding an appropriate place to smoke, some smoking refuge. Often covert behavior, as they are keeping the new habit secret. Then there's even how to light a cigarette, lighter or matches? Then there is buying more cigarettes, running around daytime, nighttime, rainstorms, snowstorms, standing outside a restaurant or place of business in what some smokers have come to call "the losers club."

As the habit is learned, and reinforced as behavior, it becomes a reaction, a break from stress, a way to mentally regroup, detaching from the moment, a maladaptive coping behavior.

Here are **some key elements** I put into every *Smoking Cessation* session/program I host:

Prior to the session, all smoking items, including cigarettes, cigars, ashtrays and lighters are now and forever thrown away.

Your client is now reconditioned into a life where they will become and forever remain, smoke-free, cigarette-free, nicotine-free. This approach can be easily adapted to people smoking vapor or chewing tobacco.

Unconditional forgiveness and release of any and all thoughts, feelings, actions, reactions, memories, modes of detaching from stress, ways of detaching from challenges related to smoking, all unproductive critical self-judgments, in ways both known and unknown, are now unstoppably being fully forgiven.

The subconscious mind is forever adaptively releasing any and all resistance, blockages, doubts, fears or any issue, including using smoking as a crutch, which might ever arise.

Their inspired mighty inner hero rises up to release and circumvent any and all challenges, which might ever arise in order to keep your client adaptively and permanently smoke-free, cigarette-free, ever vigilant, including forgiving, releasing, and easily moving beyond anything which might ever stand in the way, a forever smoke-free and cigarette-free life.

A better and more inspired vision of who they are, mentally, having risen above smoking and cigarettes, now takes shape and is encouraged to remain. And as they forever remain healthier, happier, motivated, smoke-free, cigarette-free, living a smoke-free, cigarette-free life, inner wisdom guides their way, more peaceful and joyous about this freedom. Re-identified, permanently and forever, now living life as forever smoke-free, cigarette-free, ex-smoker, non-smoker, permanently gifting themselves this life. A greater sense of unconditional love, joy, vitality, and optimism for themselves, and those you love most, including their children, their family, their spouse, all things they love. Now knowing they can succeed at this as a profound truth.

Replacing smoking sensations and feelings with sensations of clean, fresh air, inspirational feelings of victory, breakthrough, success, personal pride, and empowerment, adaptive and effective, driven forward, heroically inspired. Enjoyably drinking water and saving lots of money as replacement, should any urge arise. A more overwhelming urge, the urge to stay smoke-free, cigarette-free.

Resting better, and sleeping better through the night. Finding newer and better things to do with their hands. Becoming evermore stubbornly determined to succeed. The more they used to smoke, the more reversed this remains back upon itself, having moved 180°. The more challenged, the more obstinate and stubborn they become to remain forever smoke-free cigarette-free. Treating themselves in the way, lovingly, just as a more perfected parent would a wonderful child.

Ever improving self-perception, a powerful and even felt warm glow of heart and mind, driving ever-increasing success. Now achieving greater self-respect and self-love. An ever-growing sense of liberation and freedom. The feel of a cigarette in their hand or mouth, now just simply wrong. A greater awareness, fingers and hands and movement associated with smoking, even consciously, choosing to use their hands for something better, productive, and creative. A greater sense of self-support and determination, gaining strength every time they enjoyably reinforce via self-hypnosis, in ever-increasing results and success. Actively looking forward to self-hypnosis reinforcement, evermore enjoyable.

Just as if within any point in their lives, when they were simply finished and done with something, ready to move on, so too now with the smoking habit is outgrown, moved on from, a thing of the past, forgiving, releasing, now forever finished. Their last cigarette forever, just before their session, a sense of relief. For should there be any stumble, and instantaneous rebalance, truly, a learning experience, gained from, wiser, evermore successful.

New places, new habits, perhaps even new friends, everything reinforcing a smoke-free, cigarette-free life, forever. Their very best aspects rising up unbeatably to succeed. Perpetual, self-adaptation and reinforcement of all things known or unknown, keeping them free of smoking and cigarettes forever, while awake, while asleep, even while happy, pleasant dreams, liberated, and evermore perfecting a smoke-free cigarette-free individual. A smoke-free, cigarette-free chapter of their life right now into forever begins.

Creating a major life reset. As if going back for a moment to a younger time, a year or two before they began smoking, putting their foot down back then, and making a pivotal life choice to remain smoke-free, cigarette-free for their entire life, almost as if having remained smoke-free, cigarette-free, always. [This works extremely well, as if they never smoked in the first place, as if they remained smoke-free their entire lives].

Suggestion –

Your desire to succeed here easily grows, overwhelming any desire you once ever had to smoke, growing only ever stronger. You may even begin to wonder how easy it is to succeed at, breathing easier, feeling better, becoming better, living better, reset completely to a smoke-free, cigarette-free, longer, well-deserved, relief, healthier body and for the rest of life. While forever releasing all things unneeded, evermore completely and forever from your body, emotions, thoughts and life, as any and all of this just seems to be happening on its own, reset to accomplish only your very best, remaining happy and delighted about this, as you now know, as this time, once and for all, it's easy, and forever.

Professional Insights –
Weight Reduction/Release Insights
Personal Story –

In terms of my own weight management, some time ago I decided it was time to get rid of unwanted weight. As a professional hypnotist practicing my own self-hypnosis, and having practiced self-hypnosis most of my life, I decided to use hypnosis to get my weight down to a more manageable size.

I thought to myself, "I want to get my weight down. How am I going to do this, in ways which are effective, comfortable, in ways I can stick to? When the mind is in hypnosis, free and clear of extraneous distractions, open to improvement, information and behavioral change, then change can come, powerfully and effectively, as so my answers came to me.

My answers were: a change in my diet, and as a form of exercise, power walking with two to five pound dumbbells in my hands. I now enjoy power walking, I look forward to it, it relaxes me and clears my mind of stress. Further, I've replaced breakfast with oatmeal, a carbohydrate which seems to help me keep my weight down. Sugary drinks are now out, the majority of liquid I drink is now purified water. And as for drinking predominantly water, I'm very happy about it. Easier for me.

And yet if you approach somebody who is resistant, they are likely to say, "Water morning, noon and night, and oatmeal twice a day, oh I don't like that. I just want to eat what I want, like candy and whatever else that comes down the pike, potato chips and stuffing my face."

A great many people overeat or choose to eat the wrong foods in abundance as reward, emotional support, gaining weight as a form of emotional self-protection while ignoring body signals, which are reporting their hunger has been assuaged. So much goes on with people with eating, including conditioning from early childhood, where they must finish everything on their plate. Then there's eating socially, to binging when feeling sadness, loneliness, even happiness and celebrations, and a wide variety of other emotional issues. The fast food industry perpetuates oversized portions of food. The average supersized meal is 7 to 8 times larger than what a human being needs to consume at a meal!

I don't personally find French fries as appealing as I once did—part of my own self-hypnosis reconditioning process. And yet, prior to doing this, I used to eat waffle fries in restaurants as part of dinner, delivered on my dish in a great big pile. This was the equivalent of eating five potatoes on a dish. For the average person, if somebody said, "Eat these five potatoes" you'd likely hear, "How can I eat five potatoes?" But when it's French fries and they are being eaten without thinking, they seem to go down pretty easily. Most of your clients don't realize how much food they are actually eating! Many hypnotists I have met don't share the concept of oversized portions with their clients.

A Few Ideas Here on Snacks

Many people eat while distracted, overfeeding themselves subconsciously. If your client is an ice cream eater, often, after the first spoonful or so, they can no longer taste the flavor of the ice cream. The cold immediately starts numbing their taste buds, so very soon they are simply eating something cold. Consuming snack chips from a bag while distracted by television, a movie or a sporting event generally finds the bag empty in very little time. For many people, the container size is the serving size, a pint of ice cream then becomes one serving.

Here are **some key elements** I put into every *Weight Reduction/Release* session/program I host:

Your perception of yourself and of your body, and body image, re-identified as lighter, thinner, healthier, better, now improving. Any and all thoughts, feelings, emotions, memories, actions, reactions, adaptations whichever lead to weight gain, now dissolving, resolving, forgiven, released, releasing, as you, now ever more adaptive and effective at achieving and remaining healthier and better, lighter and thinner. Feeling emotionally better supported, fortified and protected, safe in your world, as well as within the experience you call your life. Your choices and tastes change and vastly improve in your favor.

Eating only at appropriate mealtimes, feeling fulfilled and completely satisfied.

Food is now known as sustenance, something supporting you nutritionally, more actively achieving a lifelong better body, as better habits, actions, impulses, tastes, feelings, better and more effectually responsive emotions, thoughts, powerfully now working in your favor, mind, correctly ever onward, beyond and through any and all aspects, working in greater harmony onward, better body, emotions, thoughts, actions, habits, reactions, ideas, feelings, working in harmony to take better care of you as a lighter, thinner and healthier you now and forever emerges, releasing all things heavy and unwanted, unneeded, all working in your favor, you easily moving you energetically forward into a thinner, healthier and better, more resolved you. Better and more inspired, corrected thoughts and emotions completely support you in achieving breakthrough success.

Eating more slowly and chewing more carefully, you begin to know less is more, you fill up, feeling it sooner, slowly chewing and eating your food more appropriately for better digestion. Having grown up more and doing better, refreshing water replaces old inappropriate or sugary beverages, kiddy drinks, as you are determined to remain lighter and healthier. You move away from, kiddy foods, foods intended for children, as salty, sweet, greasy food, so much more unpleasant, unappealing. You've simply yet powerfully have just grown up, moved on and have come to realize your tastes have refined and improved. You choose to do better, as healthier and better meals provide more beneficial habit adjustment or instead, health and body improvements, providing evermore appropriate nutritional support. Choosing healthier and more appropriate food now, your tastes have improved in your favor, now knowing this as fully-functioning truth. Consuming food better means providing comfort and beneficial nutrition, while always only eating free of media distractions like television and computers. Food is now slowly enjoyed and consumed, proper time allotted, consumed sustaining health and nutrition, while seated at a table, smaller plates, slowly eaten, carefully chewed, more appropriate portions, sustaining you, as a healthier and lighter, thinner you, calmer and more comfortable, now begins and lasts, lifelong. A small taste, a slowly savored taste of any food, melting into your mouth is enough to release a craving for any food.

Your desire to succeed here easily grows, always overwhelming any desire you once ever had to gain weight, hold weight or eat in any way, slowing your goals, only growing, only ever stronger. You may even begin to wonder how easy it is to succeed at melting off any and all things unneeded more completely and forever from your body, emotions, thoughts and life, as any and all of this just seems to be happening on its own, remaining happy and delighted about this, as this time, once and for all, it's easy, and forever.

Suggestion– Weight
Life and Body Reset –

It's as if someone from deep, deep inside of you, has reset a switch, a dial, a computer, or thermostat of some kind. More effectively and easily allowing you to burn food, weight, fat, calories, higher and healthier, filled up and comfortable, comfortable yet easy as you are reset and more appropriate metabolism now forever better, self-supporting a well-deserved, thinner, healthier and better you, the past forgiven and smoothly emerged from, as the thinner and healthier you forever arises.

Professional Insights –
Stress Management Insights

According to an article in a medical journal published in 1999, 97% of later-in life-illness can be traced back to and attributed to higher levels of stress earlier an individual's life.

Here's something powerful.

As hypnosis is a place opposite stress,
Stress Kills People, Hypnosis Kills Stress.

Here are **some key elements** I put into every *Stress Management* session/program I host:

- Suggesting subconscious activation of automatic deep, slow and steadying breathing whenever stressed, to generate a calming and a detachment from the stress. This a new, and forever sustainable, stress-relieving reaction.

- Choosing to respond above the stress, your client is now heroically inspired to rise above.

- Relaxing and flowing through adversity. The greater the challenge, the more slightly detached, deep-breathing, calmer and more deeply serene they become.

- Rising above the stress-filled situation, improved thought and emotional responses arise.

- Mentally stepping outside the stress situation, and now forgiving learned past reactions, creating a true sense of detachment from the moment as mental empowerment instead takes place.

- Mentally re-managing reactions, choosing to do better and differently, while keeping the smaller stuff small.

- The only power something has is the power you give to get over yourself, in this new chapter of your life; you keep your inner power within.

- Linking hypnotic rest and serenity as a more appropriate and self-perfecting reaction to stress, is now memorized as a sensation to reactivate.

- A dynamic change of perspective occurs, a shift towards relaxing through barriers, maintaining empowerment as new and better stress-relieving thoughts arise. Is today's stress going to mean anything in 10 years?

- What would the future wiser you now do? Having learned to detach, with 16 to 17 years of mastery development on rising above challenging situations later down the road?

- As if guided from on high to do better. Activating their inner master of handling stress.

- Choosing a higher, greater, better and more appropriate emotional reaction and response.

- Mentally reversing the stress energy back away from one-self.

- Maintaining one's own inner power through calming detachment, choosing a more harmonized response, responding as an adult, automatic deep breathing activation, while free of ever being swept up in any stress-filled challenging moment. Expressing calmness while challenged by stress generates a greater sense of peace and self-preservation. Winning at this game.

- Knowing when to walk away and emotionally detach. Giving the people and circumstances in any situation only the most effective, appropriate response, within your own best interest, and the very best interests of all concerned.

- Generating and keeping a thriving sense of self-preservation, and knowing you have been okay, are OK, and will be okay yesterday, today, tomorrow.

- Beginning anew as if permanently reset.

Suggestion –

Like a boulder in a fast running stream of water, the challenging adversity washing beyond and around, now polishing you. And like the water within that stream, winding up wherever it needs to go, so too does any challenge. Like a mighty river cascading down the side of the mountain in the spring, with a boulder in the center, that river, any and all challenges, stress and adversity simply flows around you and polishes you in the process, you now a mighty master of your life, better, brighter, shinier, renewed and determined to forever remain so.

While you are awake, while you were asleep, while you were dreaming happy pleasant dreams, happy pleasant thoughts overwhelm the limitations of the past, renewing and refreshing you. You more easily now, effortlessly, serene, peaceful and calm, even creatively generating this, past moments of responding now done, finished, let go of, learned from, and moved beyond. Evermore certain and sure, you are now free. Eternally remaining effective and powerfully adapting by creating better ways of relaxing your way out of and beyond any and all stressful moments.

Professional Insights –
Better Sleep/Better Rest Insights

There can be a wide variety of issues causing anyone restless nights of sleep, generating incomplete sleep. Stress still being held onto from the day's activities, a general lack of trust in life, worries mulling over in someone's mind, numerous fears, including financial issues, relationship challenges and a wide list of other issues can help to create sleep deprivation. You can also be from something as simple as remembering a few rough nights where sleep wasn't smooth or didn't come easy, and now worrying every night might just be the same.

Here are **some key elements** I put into every *Better Sleep/ Better Rest* session/program I host:

- Establishing a set time of night, to rest, a regular bedtime.

- Personal rest is well deserved, tomorrow is another day.

- Bedtimes are now free of television, computers, stress-filled telephone calls, overanalyzing, struggles, stress-filled situations and challenging people, over-stimulating food and drink, setting up a quiet and gentle time an hour or so before bed rest. One hour of unwinding to relaxing music, as a pre-bed regimen.

- Eating a sustainable meal early enough to remain hunger-free throughout their nighttime experience.

- Suggesting the release of worries one or two hours before bedtime while instilling a greater sense of trust in an individual's life experience.

- Just as it has been done so many times before, simply put your head down on the pillow, close your eyes, and go to sleep, deep sleep, just as you have on so many other nights.

- Accepting the following fact: Trusting in yesterday took care of you, today took care of you, and tomorrow will be just the same.

Forgiving and releasing everything and anything whichever once stood, will stand or might stand in the way of a wonderful night's sleep, mentally, emotionally, or in any way, both known or unknown to them. Their automatic subconscious mind is now and forever adaptively resolving and releasing any and all resistance and blockage, now and forever free.

Suggestion –

All of the day's issues and struggles, all of the day's worries and challenges, are relaxed away from and put upon a shelf, free now forever, your mind is and becomes a never stressing over these things, the day put up on a shelf an hour into each and every night before bedtime, as you simply go to bed, put your head on the pillow and just go to sleep, like thousands of times before in your past. And at bedtime each and every night, you simply put your head on the pillow, close your eyes, and sleep! Your mind is now working any and all of this out in your favor unbeatably, in the most self-supporting of ways, you know, your best friend, any and all of this working out in ways both known and unknown to you, and so it is and remains forever on each and every slow and steady breath and heartbeat.

When it's time for sleep, and it's time for bed; it's time for sleep, time for rest; time to put the day up on the shelf, time to relax, rejuvenate, and feel a blanket of soothing, healing, relaxation energy embrace you as your whole body slumps down, into an unwinding, soothing, healing, relaxation state, as the day's cares, and challenges are put up on a shelf an hour or two before bedtime, as the day is done, and you strictly allow yourself to relax and become rejuvenated by a blissful night and a deepening rest and sleep.

Just as you have done so many times in the past, you simply put your head down upon the pillow, close your eyes, and sleep, activating the well-remembered, sweet embrace of sleep; now so much more easily, on your own. Ever more easily gotten too, and more easily effective. You relax and your dreams become carefully crafted and adaptive toward working out any issues, all issues, in your favor, as you rest deeply, easily, peacefully, and naturally, well-deserved, more trusting in your life. It's as if each and every bedtime, the energy of a soothing, restful, wearying, blanket of sleep energy is comfortably snuggling gently and soothingly right up to your body, dissolving and unwinding away every muscle, relaxing your entire wearying body, peacefully calming your ever-restful mind, unwinding and relaxing your emotions, while remaining free of second-guessing, simply and easily just falling asleep, falling asleep, as better sleep cycles and patterns now emerge, flourishing forever.

Professional Insights –
Fear Freedom

Here are **some key elements** I put into every Fear Freedom session/program I host:

- Suggest subconsciously tapping off and draining away fear energy, while establishing a higher trust in life, personal, resourcefulness, the ability to transcend each challenging moment, past, present, future while rising up, resourcefully to be mighty, having grown up and moved beyond past feelings and reactions, coupled with self-support, releasing and beyond the place where fear once was.

- Inner hero activation, which is now rising to the surface. Dissolving fear with higher reality and truth.

- Rising above everything and anything that ever once stood in their way, especially the past year, and even themselves.

- The greater the fear once was, the more emboldened and mightier they become.

- All fear-based shadows dissolving in a higher Golden-white light.

- Better thoughts, better feelings, better inspiration, serenity and peace, internal wisdom and reason, moved beyond as if mastered 12, 14, 17 years ago.

- Activating feelings of victory, triumph, success, and any and all, known or unknown, self–supporting environmental factors, people, places, things, suggesting better perception of life, and trust.

Suggestion –

Beginning to realize that fear in and of itself is nothing and you are truly the mighty one. Right now, you are self-empowered, always and forever, you are ever more empowered to rise to the top and to completely relinquish and vanquish unhappy and unpleasant fear in whatever form it used to take by becoming empowered, mighty, bold, dynamic, fearless in new and more powerful fluidly adaptive ways and by unstoppably rising to the top in the most magnificent and brilliant of ways. Blockage-free, you flow ever onward in remarkable and wonderful ways, even surprising yourself at how easy this is becoming.

Those unneeded and unwanted old fears are like an empty vessel with a hole in it, they do nothing, they hold nothing, in fact, very truly, your old fears are nothing, as you are now empowered, inspired and mighty, doing all that it takes, easier and better because fantastically, you've unstoppably moved on and are free, free at long last; not because I say so but because it is the nature of your own empowered mind and spirit to do so, unstoppably and relentlessly.

Professional Insights –
Better Memory/Better Recall/Learning Enhancement Insights

It has been said over and over again, everything we've ever experienced, seen, heard, smelt, felt, remembered is all and forever stored within our subconscious minds. Information and resources are there. Our job is to liberate and activate these memories in a way which is useful and productive, to achieve better motivation, better study habits, and breakthrough success on testing.

Here are **some key elements** I put into every *Better Memory/ Better Recall/Learning Enhancement* session/program I host:

- Relaxing, and deep breathing, to open the mind more fully while reading, watching video, or memorizing, and allowing information to absorb like a sponge.

- Procrastination-free, now motivated to set and stick to a schedule of reading, study, and thinking time, time to reflect on how any system of study functions and operates.

- Bringing study habits down to levels of ridiculous ease, three minutes a day, yet once in motion, easily exceeding that. I'm finding the experience productive, enjoyable, the relaxed and open, ready to absorb mind.

- Understanding the lay of the land, the format by which any system operates. This allows for reasoning to take place, should an answer be unknown, allowing a better chance of succeeding on a test or any challenging question.

- Relaxing and allowing recall to take place, releasing struggle issues in ways profound and productive, in ways known and unknown, while instead allowing information to flow.

- Trusting in first recalled response. Trusting the first answer that comes to mind, free of overanalyzing and then changing the answer.

- Relaxing, releasing doubt, forgiving and releasing any and all emotions which ever once stood in the way, feelings of what's the use, getting past teacher/professor personality conflicts, finding something about the subject now fascinating, as well as moving beyond second-guessing, in to relaxation, an open mind able to recall, perform, reason out, and trust first instincts.

- Allowing for an *A-Ha moment* of recall by clearing and opening the mind for a moment.

Professional Insights –
Sessions for Breakup/Divorce - Heartbreak and Breakup Relief

I have hosted many sessions through the years focusing on overcoming breakups and heartbreak, designing of these sessions from a woman and man's perspective. Quite often clients call saying, "I'm getting divorced" or "I just broke up with someone. Make me forget them permanently." I've even heard, "I saw a technique somewhere where you can erase somebody's mind." I always respond, "No, the more effective and important technique involves suggesting a client give dramatically less to value to the relationship and all things connected. As if moved away from , and healed over the course of many years. In fact, so much less important, as if the breakup had occurred 17 or 19 years ago."

A Hypnotist's goal here is to get the client's subconscious mind adaptively working out and releasing thought and emotional patterns which mull over could-haves, would-haves, should-haves. Suggesting the release any and all issues, while generating greater inner peace, greater senses of personal self-worth, self-esteem, security, serenity, generating forward movement into better moments, providing a personal redefinition and reformatting into better self-supporting thought and emotional processes.

Here are **some key elements** I put into every *Breakup/Divorce - Heartbreak and Breakup Relief* session/program I host:

- A new life begins renewed.

- Free of over-dwelling, rather seeing relationship changes as a stepping stone toward better. As if the breakup happened, and has been healed 14, 16, 17, 18 years, processed, released, moved on from.

- Dilating time to accelerate heartbreak healing. A greater trust in all life aspects, supportive and better life and friendship choices. In this exciting new beginning, making life choices and having learned lessons, generating a more self-supporting life.

- Regardless of circumstances, both your client and their life is steadfastly still here, now ever more determined to make the best of life.

- Improved self-worth, self-confidence, self-esteem, and

release of negative words, thoughts, feelings, emotions, judgments upon others, self-judgments, focusing on assets and forgiving and diminishing any importance of deficits, replaced with a greater sense of unconditional self-love.

- Acceleration of emotional release, focus on inner harmony. Acceptance of the fact as the previous relationship was not meant to be, yet lessons and improvements have now been gained from. Excited looking forward toward better future moments. Finding comfort and solace within the flow of the individual's life. Alone time means quality time to love and understand better oneself, self-appreciation. Alone time is utilized to get to know and appreciate one's self better.

- Deep release of critical self-judgment is even more important than releasing judgments about their ex.

- Better thoughts, better feelings, better sensations, ever more self-supporting, while awake, while asleep, even while happy pleasant dreams perpetuate the resolve and release of any and all issues, known or unknown, generating a brighter and better future filled with more limitless opportunities, including better supportive relationships, friendships, even romance.

- More fully forgiving things said, more fully and completely forgiving things unsaid. Greater personal self-evolvement.

HYPNOTIC POWER BONUS

Insight –
A Super–Beneficial Gift – A 9–Hour Nap and a 7–Hour Back & Foot Rub

One additional aspect I want to share with you is in every private or group session I host, every speed-hypnosis demonstration, as well as every stage show I perform, is sharing a wonderful gift. The gift of suggesting the client feel as if they've had *a nine hour nap and a seven-hour back and foot rub.*

To date I have yet to meet anyone would not like blissful night of deep sleep and wonderfully calm and relaxed muscles in their back, legs and feet. Sometimes during on the spot public demonstrations I've hosted in places like restaurants, stores, hotels, airports, etc., the gift as described above is one of the most appreciated any of us can share. It is also a powerful proof of our gift of hypnosis.

It's also a good idea to suggest this gift will not interfere with a regular night's sleep.

Another useful point in this gift is to suggest the following morning when they arise from bed, they now begin in ways potent, powerful, meaningful and knowing, completely assured, their very best next chapter of their lives.

Suggestion –
A 9–Hour Nap and a 7–Hour Back & Foot Rub

As you float, drift, and dream, it is as if somehow, you just had a nine-hour nap and a seven-hour back and foot rub, muscles melting and dissolving, feeling great from head to toe, on top of the world, truly better than you have in years, as your muscles, back, legs and feet, even your emotions, thoughts, feelings, in fact all you are so deeply, truly, blissfully, beneficially relaxed and comfortable.

Later when you arrive home, you also know you will sleep peacefully and easily, even deeply right through the night, awakening the following morning with happy anticipation, somehow completely certain, serene, and sure now the very best chapter of your life begins tomorrow when you get out of bed, happy and glad, even excited, like times when you were a kid and something wonderful like your best birthday or holiday was about to happen. Driven forward, free of procrastination, you just remain thriving, succeeding, more easily realizing the very best, your every goal, living your life dynamically, even while stepping up, living your very best dreams.

Insight –
The Magic Wand Session?

A great many potential clients have contacted hypnotists requesting what I have come to call the *Magic Wand Session*.

Perhaps from a general lack of knowledge or even simply seeking to save money on session fees, these potential clients want everything done at once covering a wide variety of issues. These can include smoking cessation, weight loss, better public speaking, overcoming a fear, etc., and somehow expect us to do this all at one time.

Like most of us, I have had to explain that while I can incorporate self-esteem, self-confidence and motivational suggestions as a bonus into the sessions I host, such as smoking cessation or weight loss, being all over the map and aiming at various targets will generally not achieve spectacular results on any one issue. Most major life issues presented for sessions in and of themselves require a major amount of effort to resolve via carefully focused suggestions.

However, I did have a discussion years ago. . .

Insight –
The Everything Session

Ormond McGill and I once discussed "The Everything Session." So here's my personal gift to you. Ormond and I used to laugh about this. Ormond was one of the finest human beings I have ever met in my entire life.

If you walk away with anything from this work, this by itself can be completely useful.

"The Everything Session" could very well be used no matter what session you do.

Any skilled hypnotist potentially could do any session this way, or utilize this as a part of your overall success intervention strategy.

Give a powerful and interesting pre-talk, building rapport and using humor, and discuss what you are going to do. Then deeply hypnotize, get your client into the deepest possible trance state, insuring achievement of some deep level of REM, then . . . "Whatever has been bothering you, wherever it came from, however it manifested, it is now dissolved and evaporated," Let me add one thing . . .

Suggestion –
The Everything Session

Whatever has been bothering you, wherever it came from, whatever it was, whether any thought, feeling, idea, memory, sense, sensation, impulse, habit, action, reaction, memory, any and all, now releasing forever unwanted and useless in any way, both known and unknown to you, and however it manifested, truly now, it is now resolved, dissolved, releasing and released, and is completely evaporated far, far away from you both now and forever. Going, going, gone, and gone forever. Ahh... it feels just so great now to be right now so forever free."

SESSION PREPARATION

Technique –
Better Session Preparation Equals Better Session Success

Practically all my session work, either private or group, is prepared in advance for the best possible outcome and maximum impact via careful and precise intake.

Like a great many of us in this profession, I get contacted for private sessions by telephone and by e-mail. I normally start with "What can I do for you?"

After explaining who I am, how I got here, and a bit about how hypnosis works, it is time for a bit of information intake related to the client's challenges.

Better Information Intake for Targeted Suggestion Writing

After some careful client issue intake, generally via telephone at first, only once the session is booked I ask the client to send me via email a list of additional information l so I can carefully prepare each session private or group, scripting their personalized suggestions in advance.

Technique –
Five Short and Simple Sentences

Very specifically, I ask for five short and simple sentences, or what we once called in grammar school "sentence fragments," on the session topic. I request a short, simple list of their challenges, or weak spots which demanding improvement. In other words, what's going on? Or what's not going on? Or perhaps even better instead: What needs to be in order to achieve a better place?

I have found in my many years of service, this method is often enough to get a highly effective session properly prepared, written in advance. This way there is less shooting from the hip when delivering suggestions, or worse, having the client exit the session as additional brilliant ideas pop to mind, too late to be of any consequence.

When doing this type of intake, additional information, sentences and paragraphs *are not required*, discouraged. Some clients over the years occasionally ignore these instructions, making my wading through what they've written necessary.

Technique –
Sentence Number Six and its Value

Additionally, I also ask the client in advance for a sixth sentence utilizing this e-mail intake technique. What I request in sentence number six varies from session to session.

For smoking cessation sessions, sentence number six is: At what age did you begin smoking?

For weight loss, how many pounds do you wish to release?

For other sessions, was there some sort of trauma or turnaround in your life connected to this and if so what was it?

I review the intake hours or days before writing the session. Then via self-hypnosis, I allow my subconscious mind to begin working out the various details, personal inspirations and methods to generate, to creatively write, preparing session suggestions in advance. In other words, I let my mind start playing with what content I'm going to write in advance so when I'm ready to write, it flows out of me like water from a pipe.

When sitting down ready to craft session suggestions, I have already put myself once again into self–hypnosis, or as some might call it "in-state," with the *intent* of asking my sub-conscious mind to work efficiently and to maximum effect.

After years of practicing this technique, when my subconscious mind is ready, sometimes overwhelmingly so, I sit down and voice dictate suggestions. Through this method I have found quite often seen suggestions come pouring from my mind verbally, sometimes even faster than the voice-recognition in my computer can keep up with. So much better when the olden days with my fingers could barely keep up typing.

Using your subconscious mind to generate suggestions allows for better session preparation, higher impact, and maximum client benefit. It also alleviates the feeling, post-session, of having forgotten to add an inspired idea, which could have been contained within this session. As a hypnotist this makes *your subconscious mind* one of your most vital and valuable assets in helping clients achieve habit improvement goals.

My Final Words

As I conclude this book, I would like to personally thank you for taking the time to read my insights and suggestions. I sincerely wish you amazing success in your hypnosis practice, transforming and improving the lives of the clients whose lives you touch.

I trust and hope this book will make a remarkable difference in your session impact as a professional hypnotist while more powerfully delivering a workable upgrade to your session results, utilizing these insights and suggestions.

It is time for a major profession–wide upgrade. This work is meant to be thought of fluidly and adaptively. You might, in time, add your own insights, ideas and suggestions sparked by your inspiration, creativity and imagination.

It's always a beneficial idea to keep records of your thoughts and feelings as they come and go, mixed with creative imagination as to how you can apply all of your very best to enriching the lives of the people who seek your help and guidance.

It is my honor and privilege to write this book for both you and your clients to benefit.

Now get out there, make a difference, and light up the world!

Key Concepts

1 – Self-Perpetuation

2 - Inspiration

3 - Motivation

4 - Body

5 - Emotions

6 - Mind

7 - Time

8 - Guidance

9 - Truth

10 - Inner Hero

11 - Struggle Release

12 - Blockage Release

13 - Removing Limits

14 - New Foundations

15 - Reorientation

To contact John Cerbone and receive his newsletter, please join us at:

CerboneHypnosisInstitute.com

WorldFamousHypnotist.com

HypnosisStageShow.com

Trance-Master.com

HypnotistPro.com